Yes You Can Regain Control of Your Life and Be Happy Again

Brahim Derder

iUniverse, Inc.
New York   Bloomington

Yes You Can Regain Control of Your Life and Be Happy Again

Copyright © 2009 by Brahim Derder

iUniverse books may be ordered through booksellers or by contacting:

iUniverse
1663 Liberty Drive
Bloomington, IN 47403
www.iuniverse.com
1-800-Authors (1-800-288-4677)

ISBN: 978-1-4401-1715-2 (sc)
ISBN: 978-1-4401-1716-9 (ebk)

Printed in the United States of America

iUniverse rev. date: 01/29/2009

Table of Contents

Introduction: The Secret of Life

The ONLY Two Events of life
that we have to Deal with

Epictetus, the Greek philosopher, said "the world is divided into two realms: The things we cannot control and the things we can control. In the realm of things we can control, there is only one thing – our mind. We cannot control what other people do or say, but we can control how we react to what they do or say. "

Indeed, life is a series of events. Some of these events, during our life, are controllable (we can influence and change) and others are not controllable; they are unchangeable (we have no control, non- whatsoever, over their outcome).

We live in an environment where we encounter on a daily- basis primarily two types of events: events we cannot change, and events we can change.

In summary:

There are two major categories of events that affect our lives every day:

1) Major crises and disasters (floods, hurricanes, diseases). We usually handle these biggies (uncontrollable events) properly, because we simply ACCEPT them as they come without trying to change them; since we are convinced that we cannot change them, therefore, we just accept them and let them go of them.

2) Daily activities—hassles, frustrations, worries, problems, decisions, and difficult people whom we let bother us. We usually have a hard time dealing with these events, because we feel that we can change the outcome of these events, and because we believe that these events are controllable events. We can, to a degree, control the DAILY ACTIVITIES to an extent, not like the uncontrollable events which we have no choice but just accept them.

The key secret hinges on knowing which events we simply accept, because we cannot control them anyways, and the events which we can control. This is a dilemma sometimes, because events are not clear and categorized as controllable (events that we can influence and change), and events that we can control. In the controllable events category, for example, we know we can control our actions: To get an education or not to get an education, to get married or not to get married, to insult someone back or not-when they insult us or to let it go and not insult them back, to eat fattening foods or not, and the examples go on for the rest of our lives.

In the uncontrollable events we know, for example, that we cannot control hurricanes, earth quakes, natural death, etc. Most of the events are easy to identify, but sometimes when others are involved we get confused and we have a hard time drawing the line between the controllable and the uncontrollable events. The Serenity Prayer summarizes this thought in the following hopeful way:

God grant me the serenity to accept the things I can't change, the courage to change the things I can, and the wisdom to know the difference.

This is where the serenity prayer can be useful if we heed it and accept it.

If you believe in God then you simply accept the "assumption and /or truth" that God makes things happen for a reason always, and do not try to explain the "unexplainable"-Things that you do not understand how and why they happen such as natural disasters, death, etc.

If you do not believe in God, then realize that you are equipped with only limited resources which allow you limited control of life events, and accept it without resentment; it is better to accept all the things that we simply can't change.

Change what you can control and let alone what you cannot control. As a result, you will have peace of mind, success, and everything you want, and you will avoid all UNWANTED things such as stress, anger, frustration, and things that result from trying to do the impossible by simply accepting the UNCHANGEABLE (what you cannot change.) Trying to change the impossible will create disharmony, frustration anger, stress, and even depression and desperation, and it will rob you of joy of living which is your right. So, accept the unchangeable and be happy, and reap the joy of living.

Chapter # 1 — Set Goals

Goals: Plan, map, and set goals for your life

Goals will assist you reach success and peace of mind. Your present situations don't determine where you can go;they only determine your starting place and point. The purpose of setting goals is to focus your efforts and actions on your future. Delightful things will begin to happen when you set goals for them. Your power to accomplish becomes a reality when you set goals.

Your mind reaches toward achievement when it has clear objectives. Goals give you a starting place and a destination. Just focus your full power on your passion,and you will achieve success. Act on your dreams and they will be realized.

Setting Goals for your Life and why?

Setting goals and planning will enable you to regain joy of living in your Life. Setting goals is like drawing a map that shows you how to get from point A to point B with all the routes and turns, between point A and point B, to the final destination; your ultimate goal or objective.

Goal setting encourages one to look at themselves more clearly to see WHERE they are NOW and what they want and where they want to go in the FUTURE. This is truly helpful as it can help one see the many blessings in their lives as well as what improvements would be needed. The first step to achieving goals is by acknowledging that there is something that needs to be changed. Goal setting provides a tool kit for you to change and create the life YOU WANT, DESIRE, and DESERVE.

What Type of Goals Should You Set?

You should set goals in all areas of your life, such as your social life, your finances, your education, your career, your health, your, and so on.

Who should you set Goals For?

It is best to make goals for yourself. In addition, helping others with setting their goals is helpful to them and to you too.

When is Goal Setting Helpful?

Goal setting is always a good practice, and it is mandatory when something needs to be changed. This can be required, for example, when one is unhappy in his or her job, in his or her relationship, etc.

Some people find it useful to make goals before big events, such as marriage, changing careers or businesses, etc. Making and setting goals for the marriage, for example, often makes the relationship stronger, more unified, and successful.

Others make goals daily, weekly, monthly and/or yearly. New Year resolutions are simply goals for the New Year.

Where in Your Life would a Goal Be Helpful?

One can have any sort of goals. Common areas for goal setting, as stated already, include: health, financial, business, spiritual, relationship/family, and whatever you want to accomplish.

How Do You Create Effective Goals?

Goals that involve your PASSION really work. This is because, often there is high (positive) emotion, desire, and strong images related to your set of goals. Being able to picture and imagine a goal really does help achieve it.

Goals, with dates, in fact help the materialization process. Adding a picture, and deep desire really make it happen. Use your imagination to visualize attaining the goals and its rewards.

Goal Topics: once aagin, people create goals based on their list of values.

This can be one's health, family, spiritual practice, relationships, work, or livelihood. Sometimes it is obvious that something is not working in your life. If this is the case, focusing on what you like in that part of your life to be like, is an excellent place to start.

Imagining a supportive network of family and friends or an extremely satisfying job that leaves you energized are great examples of such goals.

Other times, people just have a restlessness or uneasiness about their lives. Often this is due to having a life that is not fulfilling, and the solution to this anxiety is simply SETTING definite goals.

Write them down, and then go at acting on achieving them by simply doing the necessary work, because- as the adage states- doing the TALK (writing your goals) is not enough; it is doing the WALK (acting on your set goals) that counts.

Creativity will help you set goals and succeed in your life

Creative people enjoy making something out of nothing. Part of being creative is by setting goals. Most people who are successful in life are successful because they set goals and develop step-by-step action plans for achieving them. Unfortunately, only few adults (about five or less percent) have clear, written goals. Especially considering that those who do set goals accomplish up to 10 times more than other people, including people who are more talented. In fact, a person who sets goals - and focuses on taking small steps to achieve them - will run circles around a genius *who talks a lot but never does anything*. In fact about fifty percent of those who set New Year's resolutions give up by the end of January, and a full half of all resolutions are abandoned within three months. So, if you want to make this year your best creative year yet - and actually stick to your resolutions - it's time to set goals and adhere to them persistently. Do something that moves you closer to your goal everyday; just do something, even very small, because it will add up and accumulate.

Setting Goals Secrets

I: decide on what you WANT:

The first step in setting your goals is to decide on what you really want to focus your attention on. Select as many things as you want, but limit your goals to specific areas such as: Health, Education, Career, Family, Social Life, etc.

II: write down your goals:

Once you've decided which things you want to focus your attention on, the next step is turning each of them into a goal.

Goals must be:

1- Passionate: Passionate goals are easy to understand and use, and ignite your passion.

2- Measurable: Measurable goals define the exact outcome you want to achieve: publish a book, complete a class in a specific area.

3- Active: Active goals use action words such as publish, draw and paint. They tell you exactly what it is you're supposed to do, rather than how it is you're supposed to feel.

4- Reachable: Reachable goals are realistic. They can actually be achieved.

5- Timed: Finally, your goals need deadlines, a specific time by which you'll achieve them: by the 30th of December, for example.

Now that you understand what makes a goal achievable, rewrite each of your goals making sure that it's clear, measurable, active, reachable and timed.

III: create an action plan:

Now that you know exactly what it is that you want to accomplish, the next step is creating a step-by-step action plan for getting it. Break big goals into smaller goals, then think of each of your goals as the rungs of a ladder. Every small goal you complete means you climb one more rung on the ladder of your success. The more steps you take, the closer you are to the top - and to achieving the creative life of your dreams.

To develop your own goal ladder, make a list of all the things you need to do to reach your goal. Put them in order, beginning with the first step and so on, and give yourself a deadline for each step. And for good measure, share your goals and your action plan with someone you trust. Having someone else to whom you feel accountable will help you feel more accountable to yourself.

Celebrate your success:

When you achieve a goal, celebrate your success. Buy a new DVD; Take a hot bath, schedule a weekend away, etc. Better yet, enlist someone else who can help you. For instance, ask a friend to take you to a movie or treat you to lunch, or ask your partner to do the grocery shopping for the week or fill your car with gas for a month. And remember to reward yourself along the way, perhaps every time you climb another rung of your ladder. These rewards will fuel you to take the next step - and will help you stay focused on achieving your goals.

By following this process you'll no longer fret over and worry about failed resolutions. Instead, you'll be in the goal getters and achievers hall of fame.

The power of goal setting- Dream Big

What is true for the general and average population is also true for the creative people. There's only one way to ensure that hopes and dreams become real and that's by setting goals. A goal is something you want, of course. But, there's more to it than that. It's also something you're willing to work toward, whether it takes days, weeks, months, or years to achieve. In essence, goals are the stepping-stones that make your dreams become real. So, dream, and dream big.

You are Free to Dream Big:

Always dream big. Don't worry about whether you have the time, talent or money to achieve your dreams. Just write down whatever comes to mind. If you're having trouble completing your goals, imagine yourself 10 or even 50 years older. What if you only had six months to live? Think long-run, with a vision. Do not be short sighted; do not just look for immediate gratifications- always have a long term vision. The size of your goals depends on the size of your dreams. Some goals can be achieved in a day, a week or a month. These are short-term goals. For example, taking a class on how to type is a short term goal. Other goals - such as becoming a doctor or a business person can take much longer, perhaps years, even decades. These goals are called long-term goals. It's important to have both kinds of goals.

Chapter # 2 — Take Action: Nothing happens without action

Acting and making things happen- Do it now (DIN)

"Whatever we learn to do, we learn by actually doing it; men come to be builders, for instance, by building, and guitar players by playing the guitar: By doing self-controlled acts, we come to be self-controlled; and by doing brave acts, we become brave."

Aristotle, Greek philosopher "A life of reaction is a life of slavery, intellectually and spiritually. One must fight for a life of action, not reaction."

Rita Mae Brown

"You could march an army through the gap that separates *action* from *reaction*. It's all about control. If you're reacting, someone else is in control - pulling your strings and dictating what you say and do. But if you're acting, you're in control - you've taken the strings off and are directing your own show. Think of it this way: You either have action or you have Reaction and all that it brings with it, as in: Reproach, regret, Repentance, Remorse, Repine, and Resentment. Make each moment count double"

Unknown author

"The biggest benefit came when I realized I was reacting to my own feelings and emotions."

Jim Palermo

Take action to succeed in your life

Acting after planning and setting goals is required so you can Regain control of Your Life and Be Happy Again. A thought is the seed of any success ever known to mankind. For example, all the inventions and discoveries accomplished by man- from the invention of the wheel to modern computers, the internet, etc- started with an idea in somebody's mind. Think and ask yourself right now: where am I going? In others words, ask yourself: where am I going and how am I doing in my projects? Where am I going in my current relationship? Where and how am I doing in my current job? In my business? In my life, in general? If you do not know where you are going you will be like a ship in the middle of the ocean with no specific direction. It will end up anywhere; probably on the rocks destroyed, because of its lack of direction. You must set your goals and have a plan for your life to succeed, and succeed you will when you do what it takes.

To succeed, in summary, you must do the following:

1) Think about what you want.

2) Set goals.

3) Plan action steps to accomplish what your goals are.

4) Take action to complete the steps you outlined above.

Without action nothing happens. You must harness all your mind potentials. It has been stated that most people use less than 4% of their brain power and potentials. You must use what knowledge you already possess. Use what knowledge you have, and if indeed you need some more, then by all means acquire it quickly, and get on with activating and effectuating your plan. Just do not fall into the trap of "I need more information to act". This will make you a non-active, - non practical person, because you always think that you need some more information to act. So just do it now. Having a well thought out and defined plan and its action steps lead us to the only conclusion and that is action and ultimately to success and happiness. Having a definite purpose will help you concentrate; develop self-reliance and confidence, enthusiasm, initiative, imagination, and all the components necessary for success.

When you draw a specific plan and its action steps you basically separate an area in your life for action and specialization. Time must be allotted to achieving their actions on a day-to-day basis.

You will also be able to identify opportunities pertaining to your success because you know what you are looking for specifically and not in generalities.

Use the KFC formula to succeed and accomplish your purpose and goals.

KFC stands for KNOW what you want, FIND out and determine what you are getting so far, and if you are not getting WHAT you want CHANGE what you are doing until you get what you want.

In a nut shell:

KFC = Know what you want + Find out what you are getting + Change what you are doing if you are not getting what you want.

Decision-making is another skill that becomes natural once you have your plan and its action steps defined. The secret, however, to decision making lies in having courage in taking risks and not being afraid. Fear is the enemy of success and the cause of many failures. Therefore, make any decision with the facts you have right now and correct your decision later if needed, because waiting for all the facts to come in will be a wait forever.

Have faith and believe in what you are doing. Believing in what you are doing will give you a positive attitude towards your goals, and free you from the limitations of doubt, discouragement, indecision, and procrastination. Think, make plans; set goals, outline action steps and EXCUTE (ACT) on your action plans. Just do it; do not be intimidated; you will regain the joy of living in your life when you earn the credit of doing things.

How to Motivate Yourself to Take Action

Motivating ourselves and others is at the heart of any successful endeavor. The following are examples of getting motivated for action, and the benefits of taking action:

1) Acting or even pretending to act precedes getting in the mood. I make myself sit down at my desk, then, I pick up a pencil and go through mechanical motions of writing. I put down anything and sooner or later without my being conscious of it, my mind gets on the right track.

2) Most of the good ideas come from just getting to work.

3) Action precedes all things—nothing starts by itself.

4) Don't postpone getting started.

5) Mechanical action defeats fears. People who get things done in this world don't wait for the spirit to move them, they move the spirit.

6) People place confidence in the person who acts. They naturally assume (s) he knows what (s) he's doing.

7) Waiting for the perfect set of conditions is a wait forever. Nothing man-made can be absolutely perfect.

8) The test of a successful person is not an ability to eliminate all problems before they arise, but to meet and work out difficulties when they arise

9) In any activity, cross bridges when you come to them, because you can't eliminate all risks.

10) Action feeds and strengthens confidence. Action cures fear and gains confidence. To fight fear, act. To increase fear, wait.

11) Ideas have value only when acted upon.

12) Don't waste time getting ready to act. Start acting now instead.

Healing comes from action not from Lethargy (no action)

In conclusion, if nothing is ventured, then nothing is gained. Choose to stop using the old ways that do not work. Stop going back to the same people. If something is not working do something about it. We must try until we get it right. Unfortunately some of us limit ourselves—out of a need for security, for example. The more choices we have in life, the scarier it can be. Therefore, we eliminate choices by patronizing the same restaurant, holding the same job, following the same daily routine. Just do it now, because if nothing is ventured, then nothing is gained.

When you try doing whatever you think you should be doing, then even if you fail you know you tried at least, and you will feel good, and not guilty. Your joy of living will increase in proportion directly with your actions and efforts.

Make a Difference in your Life Time, Only Actions Matter at the end; Do It Now (DIN) What really matters at the end of your Life

When you leave this world, or rather before you leave for good- do it today- ask yourself one question: What difference did I make so far in my life? What's different now in this world because I was here on earth? And the answer to that question will be the difference that you made.

All of our intentions, thoughts, and feelings won't matter anymore when we are on our deathbeds asking that question. What will matter are the action we took and the difference that it made.

Yet we continue to obsess about our thoughts and become fascinated with our feelings. We are offended by other people. We want to prove we are right. We try to make other people look wrong. We are disappointed in some people and resent others. But, NOTHING except action will be all that matters at the end.

We could have made a difference every hour, every day, every month, and every year, if we had wanted to. So how do we do that? How do we motivate ourselves to get into action? How do we live a life of action difference-making?

The ancient philosophers, such as Aristotle, had the answer thousands of years ago: The answer lies in motion and action. The answer lies in movement, and not in lethargy.

Aristotle knew, also, how to create a worthwhile self through movement and action. He once said this: "Whatever we learn to do, we learn by actually doing it; *men* come to be builders, for instance, by building, and guitar players by playing the guitar: By doing self-controlled acts, we come to be self-controlled; and by doing brave acts, we become brave."

Just act and live a life of action by simply effectuating and making things happen. There is an old story that categorizes people into three types: the first type is the few- unfortunately only FEW- people who are engaged and engrossed into MAKING things happen and acting in general. The second type of people are the kind that simply stands by or sits down and watches others do things; they just WATCH what is happening in this world around them, and basically do nothing. The third type of people is the kind that ironically and unfortunately do nothing, nor do they even watch what is happening. In fact, they are the type that has no idea what is happening. This is the type that is totally lost and is wondering what the hell happened, when everything is all done. The first type, the doers, is the ones who enjoy life every day as if it were their last day on this earth. Act, and enjoy life as if it is your last day (it might be!); with passion, zest, gusto, and hope; no matter what you encounter every day, because solving daily problems and dealing with all its various challenges is what makes life worth living and enjoyable. Someone said life without challenges is like death, so enjoy your daily challenges.

You must earn your self-esteem
by making things happen

Self- esteem is not an empty word; self- esteem is a deed and an accomplishment.

There are two contradicting views and theories regarding self-esteem: Where and how you get it and how to keep it once you get it.

1. The old theory might state something like this:

Don't dwell on your own misfortune. Try instead to become creatively absorbed into outside interests and external activities. Stop obsessively contemplating your own navel and self. Develop rewarding interpersonal relationships. Get your mind off yourself. If you merely focus attention elsewhere, then your self-centered emotional problems will die of neglect.

At first glance, this might sound good and plausible. This approach asks us to focus on external forces and not our internal ones.

2. The new theory might go like this:

Stop worrying about other people. Try instead to build up your own sense of self-worth. Take pride in yourself.

Work toward elevating your own self-respect and enhancing your self-image. Your feelings of unhappiness and depression will surely evaporate if you only esteem yourself more highly.

These two approaches complement each other. Because we interact with the outside world, therefore, the outside world affects us as we also affect it- it is a continuous interaction. But, we also interact and contemplate our own internal selves.

Let's begin with a precise definition of terms. When we say that an individual has self-esteem - or self-respect, self-love, self-admiration, or self-worth -we do not mean that he values himself without proposed justification. We do *not* mean, in other words, that his self-esteem is unearned or unconditional. The truth is that *people tend to view themselves positively for a reason,* usually because they perceive, correctly or incorrectly (temporarily at least until they discover the truth about themselves), that they possess admirable personal traits (e.g., intelligence, creative talent, physical attractiveness) or because they indeed have enjoyed outstanding personal achievement (e.g., graduated from college, married well, or landed a prestigious job).

Self-esteem, it appears, comes through perceived individual accomplishment or through supposed possession of desirable personal characteristics.

A businessman may enjoy self-esteem because, from his viewpoint, he is professionally successful and treats his family well. A teenage girl boasts her self-esteem because she earned straight *A's* on her report card and made the varsity cheerleading squad. A politician may feel self-esteem because he won a landslide victory in the last election and sponsored a popular congressional bill to help his constituents. *There is virtually always a direct correlation between an individual's evaluations of his traits or achievements and his appraisal of his self-value and sense of worth.* In conclusion, self-esteem must be earned in a practical way in order for it to be sustained.

Chapter # 3 — Get along with others

Interdependence

Others can affect you: interdependence is part of life
It is better to get other people to
like you than dislike you

Extensive research, and even common observation, proves that people choose who they like. They marry who they like, not the ones they do not like, they vote for whom they like, and spend good times with whom they like and feel comfortable with. The benefits of being liked are infinite. The more you are liked the happier you are, and the easier your life will be.

It is also a fact that most, if not all people, like to be popular and LIKED by others. The goal of being LIKED begs the question of how to be or become likeable (liked.)

So, how and what to do to become LIKEABLE (liked by others)?

The best news for everyone is that anyone CAN become likeable by learning the L factor (Likeability factor). It is summed up in four elements that you can change and enhance:

1- Friendliness: The ability to communicate with others in a pleasant (likeable way) and open manner.

2- Realness: Simply being who you are and not pretending to be someone else. Your integrity and authenticity are manifested in your actions, and they speak for themselves.

3- Empathy: Your ability to identify, recognize, and experience others' feelings and emotions.

4- Relevance: Your true interest and capacity in connecting and relating to others' needs, wants, and issues.

It is simply your TRUE sympathy with others, under-standing of their issues, and your compassion.

You can use the acronym:

FRERE = Friendliness + realness + Empathy + Relevance =F + R + E + RE (frère means brother in French) to remind yourself of the four elements of likeability.

Famous Quotes for Taking Responsibility

1- "To decide, to be at the level of choice, is to take responsibility for your life and to be in control of your life."

Author: Abbie M. Dale

2- "To give up the task of reforming society is to give up one's responsibility as a free man."

Author: Alan Stewart Patton

3- "We must exchange the philosophy of excuse- what I am is beyond my control- for the philosophy of responsibility."

Author: Barbara Charline Jordan (b. 1936), American politician, spokesperson, US representative.

4- "Only I can change my life. No one can do it for me."

Author: Carol Burnett.

5- "Dedication and responsibility, far beyond the laws governed by man, releases the power within you, to attain all the wisdom of the universe."

Author: Christine Lane.

6- "Action springs not from thought, but from a readiness for responsibility."

Author: Dietrich Bonhoeffer.

7- "Nothing strengthens the judgment and quickens the conscience like individual responsibility."

Author: Elizabeth Cady Stanton.

8- "Responsibility is the thing people dread most of all. Yet it is the one thing in the world that develops us, gives us manhood or womanhood fiber."

Author: Frank H. Crane, American writer.

9- "We are made wise not by the recollection of our past, but by the responsibility for our future."

Author: George Bernard Shaw, Irish-born British playwright, founder "Fabian Society".

10- "It is not only for what we do that we are held responsible, but also for what we do not do."

Author: Jean Baptiste Poquelin Molière French playwright.

11- "Character--the willingness to accept responsibility for one's own life--is the source from which self-respect springs."

Author: Joan Didion.

12- "I believe that every right implies a responsibility; every opportunity an obligation; every possession a duty."

Author: John Davidson Rockefeller, Jr. American oil magnate, philanthropist.

13- "Friendship is always a sweet responsibility; never an opportunity."

Author: Kahlil Gibran, Lebanese-born American mystic poet, painter.

14- "I believe that all of us have the capacity for one adventure inside us, but great adventure is facing responsibility day after day."

Author: William Gordon, American religious leader.

15- "The price of greatness is responsibility."

Author: Sir Winston Leonard Spenser Churchill, British prime minister, author.

Take Responsibility, Blame Nobody; Regain Power, and Joy of Living

All humans shirk and avoid their responsibilities sometimes in their lives. This happens in many ways and scripts such as: It's not my fault, it's your fault. I didn't do it, and I am going to make you suffer even if I have to destroy my life in the process. It is like a game. The game is to look *for* any person, place, or thing and make them responsible for what is going on *(or* not going on) in your life. It's a game where nobody wins. It's a game where you keep bumping up against the same walls as you struggle to find someone who is the cause of your discomfort and discontent.

To have the best year of our lives, we are going to have to stop blaming others for the condition of our lives. To the extent that we blame others for any circumstance, even if we believe it to be their fault, we diminish our power to make the changes we are craving to make. Blaming has become the disease of our time. It sets us up to be victims, which then renders us powerless over our circumstances. When we are feeling stressed, drained, or resigned, we can be certain that we have fallen into victim consciousness and made another person responsible for our reality. Anything we say, think, or do that points to someone else renders us powerless.

Once you realize you are living as a victim in any area of your life, the next step is simple: Notice who you are blaming, and then stop it. Claim responsibility for your own life. No matter what another has done to you, if you continue to blame them, you will, unfortunately, lose the game. Even if you were taught to hold on and to cling-to your grudges, I urge you to give them up now. If you don't, you will have no other option than to drag the past into the future and continue down paths that lead you somewhere other than where you really want to go. Creating the best future of your life requires you to stand tall, accept 100 percent responsibility for yourself, and move forward, regardless of what others are or aren't doing. The Blame Game is always a losing game. Taking responsibility will enable you to regain your power and joy of living.

Control your Weakness or someone else will: the ABCs of Button Pushing

We have a choice between controlling our emotions or letting others control us. They can control us by knowing which of our buttons to push and when. Others, especially those who know us well, tend to use what affects us to either help us or to hurt us.

It is up to us to do or not to do something. *We always have a choice in how to react to the outside forces or stimuli.* Most of us are like machines with several buttons labeled: Anger, Outrage, Happiness, Frustration, Vengeance, etc. People selectively push any button they wish, and we mostly respond according to the pushed button. In other words, we depend on what others do or say to us.

This dependency on what others do or not do to us or for us must be eliminated and we must take charge of our reactions and not let others control our buttons (our emotions, in other words). We must choose not to let others push our buttons as they please, and even when they do we must remain serene and unaffected. It has been determined that it is not WHAT happens in our lives that affects us positively or negatively, but it is HOW we react to it and HOW we perceive it. My mother, God rests her soul, used to say whenever somebody in my house breaks something: Good; something wonderful is about to happen because of this incident. Basically, she sees something good in a bad situation, and believe it or not everyone would laugh and smile. Compare this reaction to someone else who would say: What the hell, how clumsy can you be! Take note that nothing will change what had happened.

In order to keep others and events from pushing our buttons, we must start by figuring out what or who really causes and triggers (the cause / activating event) our reactions in the first place.

There are two activating events:

1) Major crises (floods, hurricanes, diseases). We usually handle these biggies properly.

2) Daily activities—hassles, frustrations, worries, problems, decisions, and difficult people whom we let bother us and push our buttons.

It is a simple cause and effect problem: A is the cause. B is our perception. C is our reaction (based on our perception- B).

For example: A (cause or event): on the road home and in the middle of heavy traffic, someone rudely cuts in front of you abruptly without proper signaling.

B (your perception): You take this event as a personal insult, and you take it personal.

C (your reaction) you get angry. You sound your horn in protest and drive very fast to pass them and give them the finger to show them that nobody can mess with you. This incident escalates eventually into a bad accident and serious injuries to you and others, or perhaps even death that might include you and or many others.

In this particular case, C represents two things: your feelings and behavior in this specific situation that occurred at point A.

The series of events from cause, perception, and effect (reaction) can be summed up as follows:

A- Activating event: specific situation or people: The car cutting unexpectedly in front of you.

B- Your beliefs about activating events (your perception): Violated and disrespected PERSONALLY.

C- Your reaction and behavior (your response): Anger, vindication, and rage.

This is a chain of events:

At point A we had a driver who rudely cut in front of us (causing event).

At point B, this event (A) led us to our CHOSEN feeling (EMOTION) of being violated and angry. At point C, we CHOSE to REACT by following the driver and teaching him or her a lesson.

At Point B we had a choice to do one of two things: THINK that this event was not worth pursuing and let it go and keep driving, or THINK that we were violated and pursue the driver seeking vengeance. We had a choice. Therefore, the way we think in response to a specific person or situation will largely determine both our response (emotionally and behaviorally) at C, and whether we let A push our buttons, or not.

Therefore, A's don't cause C's. B's (your reaction and perception) cause C's. Clearly, it is up to you to ignore this incident at point B and avoid all the ensuing problems or to make an issue out of it and accept all the bad consequences.

However, it is not always possible to avoid all situations or people; there are instances where confrontation is a must and avoidance only makes things worse. So, what is there to do about these special cases: the answer is to have a plan of action such as the following test plan:

Test plan—instead of avoiding people and situations that push your buttons, deliberately approach these situations and desensitize yourself to button pushers.

We must understand how we upset ourselves to control our reactions, and how to change our overreactions.

At point B we have 3 beliefs (perceptions):

1) Catastrophic thinking—we make things bigger than they are. (What if….) causes many catastrophic thoughts: What if he does not love me anymore? Solution: Figure the worst outcome of "what if…" and accept it.

2) Absolutist thinking: I must, I should, I've got to, I need to, I have to, I ought to, etc. Parents, the general media (TV, books, movies, etc), teachers, friends, and others instill these habits in us.

3) Rationalization (under reactions): they are poor attempts to deny or play down what is happening. We try to make sense of or to justify our questionable behavior.

We must have realistic preferences and choices instead of primitive and instinctive reactions. They are hard to implement but possible.

Ten (10) Bad Push Buttons

a. Worrying too much about what others think of us. Excessive worrying creates a strong anxiety

b. Fear of failure: If I fail it's terrible and I cannot stand it.

c. Low frustration tolerance—people and things should always turn out the way I want them to—and if they don't it is horrible and I can't stand it.

Blame others: if I'm not respected, if I fail, or if things don't go my way I'll always blame someone else for it.

e. If I worry obsessively about some event things will turn out better.

f. Perfect solutions exist for every problem and I must find them—no such thing.

g. It is easier to avoid difficult situations and responsibilities than to face them.

h. If I never get seriously involved in anything, and maintain a detached perspective, I will never be unhappy.

i. My past (childhood, love relationship, job) is what is causing me to feel and act this way now.

j. Bad people and things should not exist and they are the cause of my disturbance.

Change your irrational thinking. This requires: commitment, awareness, and practice.

Awareness entails what I am thinking to myself about myself, and about others.

Commitment is adhering and sticking to whatever we want to change consistently and persistently, in a relentless manner.

Couples as Button Pushers

1) Couples always assume some expectations from each other. He or she must change.

2) Measure of a relationship's success: the ability to resolve differences, conflicts, problems, differences in opinion/values/ wants/preferences/priorities is the critical factor.

Five factors for a good relationship:

1) Communication: ability to discuss (as opposed to fight and argue) to solve the problem.

2) Sense of humor

3) Commitment: no other relationship is more important

4) Flexibility: being able to admit one's mistakes and change position or view.

5) Love and respect each other.

How to Stop Playing the Blame Game

Recognize and spot where in your life you are blaming someone else for your circumstances and allow yourself to see how much more power you would have if you took 100 percent responsibility for your life.

Make the following your motto and mantra:

"I am Responsible, therefore, I have the Power t o Control my Life the way I want". Repeat the following to enhance your joy of living:

I have complete control of my life, and I am responsible for everything that happens in my life time. Whatever happens in my life is under my control not anybody else's responsibility. I take full charge of all events that occur, and I am not blaming anyone for anything bad that might happen to me; I simply will take corrective actions and move on with my life. I am not blaming my parents or spouse or teachers or anybody else for anything that happened or will happen, because blaming others will only disempower me (take power from me and make me feel that others are the cause, and that means since they caused it they and only they CAN change it and correct it).

It is a fact that I am responsible for all events that happened and all events that will happen in all my life, and since I am responsible for causing them, then I HAVE the POWER to make any changes in my life events any way I wish and desire. I am starting and initiating actions regarding all aspects of my life today, and I am going to be responsible for all required actions and their results. I am not going to blame anybody else. If my actions lead to the results I want, then that is done and case is closed, but if my actions do not lead to what I want, then, I will TAKE IMMEDIATELY corrective actions and make the REQUIRED CHANGES. I feel that not taking responsibility for my own life is the same as relinquishing (giving up) my personal power to others. It is just like and similar to the following scenario: While driving to my predetermined destination (for example while I am driving to school) I stop and ask somebody else to drive my car without even telling him or her where I am going and which route I like to take. Notice how I became the passenger with no control of my destination, and how someone else became in the driver seat; in complete control of my present life events (going to school). Although, it is true that if I told the driver that I am going to school, and which route I wanted to take to get there, I COULD get there, but THERE IS NO GUARRENTEE that the driver (others) will do what I wanted. This is the essence of TAKING responsibility for all my actions and mapping my own life the way I want. Blaming others will not empower me, but taking control of my destiny by assuming all responsibilities will lead to more joy of living.

Invalidations- put- downs and insults by others

What is invalidation?

Invalidation is to reject, ignore, mock, tease, judge, control or diminish someone's *feelings*. Constant invalidation may be one of the most significant reasons a person with high innate (natural and inborn) emotional intelligence suffers from unmet emotional needs later in life.

Invalidation starts early in childhood

A sensitive child who is repeatedly invalidated becomes confused and begins to distrust his own emotions. He fails to develop confidence in himself or herself and fails to develop healthy use of his or her emotions. The working relationship between his thoughts and feelings becomes twisted. The emotional processes which worked as a defense for him as a child will probably work against him as an adult. This very commonly phenomon occurs with children, when they take on the characteristics of their parents and siblings.

The impact of Invalidation on Relationships, Work, and life in general

It is also very frequent in relationships where one partner adjusts to match the other's expectations. And, of course it happens at work too. When our goals are suppressed by another - however well meant - it is eventually life destroying. Negative evaluations (personal criticisms, opinions) by another especially at times of stress can cause extreme upset and emotional turmoil.

What to do about invalidation?

The most important aspect of handling invalidation is finding and knowing yourself and then becoming whole (complete). One of the factors that causes fragmentation of your identity and causes self-doubt - who you think and feel you are - is invalidation, which happens when you feel made wrong and mistreated by another's comments or actions.

How invalidation works and gets its grips on you

When you act according to the will of another person and suppress your own wishes, you have identified a part of yourself with the other person. You have let them into your mind, as your master to control your thoughts. You have become fragmented. One of the main ways this comes about is through invalidation, or putdowns. If somebody says your effort was 'not good enough' or that you 'shouldn't have done that', then you start to question and doubt yourself. You begin to introspect and ask 'Is there something wrong with me?' When another person wrongly evaluates or misunderstands your communications or your state of mind, naturally this is upsetting. It means the other has not understood you. Your enthusiasm wanes. You may accept this false evaluation - perhaps because of the authority or dominance of the other person. If you ignore your own feelings and believe they must be right, you begin to follow their will and attempted spill, not your own will. A part of you has identified with the other person and split from the real you.

Invalidation and its impact on even the richest people

Most of us wonder why the populations in the world who seem to have the greatest mobility and most material possessions are suffering from the bondage of despair and depression. One of the biggest causes is invalidation. As human beings we need to be both independent and interdependent. We need to feel a sense of love and of contribution (worthiness). If either (love or worthiness) are missing we become sad, we become defeated, we become joyless- without joy of living; joie de vivre as the French people say.

Invalidation kills confidence, creativity, individuality... and if we do not find a way to re-empower our individual and collective lives and to connect with our humanity it will slowly erode all that we have built into a tower of sand.

The Solution

The solution that we seek in our lives in general such as in our work and in our relationships does not lie outside us but within us. We each have the power to move past invalidation by igniting the power of our heart to touch our mind and infuse our life and the lives of others with validation, acceptance, and joy of living by being accepting ourselves despite any invalidation.

You always have choices. If a mugger threatened you with a gun, you have the choice not to give him your wallet. He might have killed you or given up and run away. But you had the choice. You may have chosen to give him your wallet, which may have been wise. But you never have to do anything against your will. You can always choose.

How to handle invalidations

There are many and various ways you might have been put-down by others and as a result agreed to have less power. You need to look again at what happened and ask yourself:

What choices did I make?

Consider the following choices:

What did I decide about myself?

What did I decide about the other person or other people?

What did I choose to think?

How did I choose to feel? What emotion did I choose?

What did I choose to do?

How did my choices affect my behavior going forward?

What other choices could I have made? And what might the effect of each of those choices be?

What positive learning can I get from this experience?

The positive learning is basically whatever insight you have found after realizing you have chosen one direction, you can revise that choice if you want and change it.

The result of being insulted and invalidated can be devastating to our ego or totally harmless; it all depends on HOW we react to the invalidation.

Chapter # 4 — Manage yourself, you are the boss in charge of your life

Self control

You can control yourself, and you can make a difference
by Changing what you can

"Only I can change my life. No one can do it for me."

Carol Burnett.

Take care of your inner child

There is a little child within each one of us:

After we are born we go through different stages of growth in our growing up process. Growing up means taking full responsibility for loving and successfully nurturing the Inner Child that lives deep within you. No matter how well or how poorly the parenting people in your life did their jobs, the challenge of nurturing yourself successfully is yours once you grow beyond childhood and adolescence.

Instead of growing up and taking responsibility for your nurturing, you may have sought instead to nurture others, hoping that they will reciprocate by tending to your needs and feelings. This model, which both women and men in our culture are scripted to follow, creates painful, guilt ridden, disappointing relationships. It serves to keep us get stuck and frustrated, loving others too much, while neglecting ourselves. Resentfully, but valiantly, we may keep on martyring ourselves and willingly keep suffering, trying to control other people's lives, while refusing to take charge of our own. Exhausting ourselves in efforts to control what we cannot control, we abuse ourselves and ignore our responsibility to ourselves which we can control.

Nurturing yourself successfully means loving, acknowledging, and accepting the Inner Child that is the essence of who you are. It also means focusing and centering the power of your mind in the energy of love so you think clearly, positively, and constructively. When you develop a truly loving, nurturing parent for yourself, allied with a healthy, positively focused mind, your Inner child will thrive in the internal climate of unconditional love and acceptance you create moment by moment for yourself. Moreover, your internal world of love and positive energy will be reflected in your outer world in loving, productive relationships with others. As you know and experience that you can take care of yourself adequately and happily, you won't be tempted into loving others too much while they neglect their responsibilities for themselves and their commitments to you.

Your external relationships mirror the quality of your relationship with yourself. If you are having difficulty in your relationships with others, you can allow those relationships to teach you about what is happening inside you among the various parts of yourself. Chances are you are acting out those inner relationships in your behavior patterns with other people.

Other people need to express themselves honestly and be loved, acknowledged, and accepted by you. They need to know you will be honest with them and say no to them when no is what you feel. They need to know you will say how you feel and what you need and release them to respond honestly, whatever their response may be. Moreover, you need to know they will reciprocate, honestly telling you what they need and feel, and releasing you to respond in the way that fits for you.

In a similar way, your Inner Child needs to know it is loved, acknowledged, and accepted unconditionally by you. It wants to be listened to, honored, and parented effectively. It is most comfortable when it can trust you to give it protection by thinking clearly and lovingly, and saying no to the fearful, critical thinking, self sabotaging parts of you. It needs to know you will say no to others when that is necessary to honor your child's legitimate needs and feelings. Your Inner Child also needs to trust that you will say no to it when its demands are excessive, when it thinks it has to have exactly what it wants immediately and when it tries to con you into doing what is not in your best interests.

It is helpful to picture the little child within you. You may want to find pictures of yourself as a child. You can have ones that you particularly like enlarged and put them in places where you will see them frequently and be reminded to remember your inner child in the present. Probably you will be most attracted to pictures of yourself when you were happy and obviously enjoying life. Seeing the Happy child clearly is important. Cherish these pictures and keep them close to your heart.

If your parents helped you learn to express yourself in healthy ways when difficult, disappointing experiences rocked your world, you probably are carrying little pain from the past forward into the present and future. Unfortunately, this has not been our cultural norm, given the fear and denial of feelings that have existed for years. It is more likely that you learned to hide and then ignore the hurt child within you while being overly sensitive to that same hurt child part in others. If so, one of your challenges as an adult is to face your own Hurt Inner Child instead of neglecting it while trying to heal its counterpart in others. Once you find the courage to turn within and look at this part of you in a nurturing attitude of love and acceptance, you are on the way to healing yourself and making yourself and your relationships whole and healthy.

But, in order to see your Hurt Inner Child, you will have to look behind the walls you have erected to hide this painful part of yourself. There are many ways to conceal the hurt child within you. Perhaps you will recognize some of these patterns in your repertoire for disguising Your Hurt Inner Child. Do you hide your hurt little child?

1. Behind a tough guy and macho facade?

2. Behind a superwoman, invulnerable exterior?

3. Behind an angry, blaming stance with others?

4. Behind compulsive behavior like overeating, alcohol and drug abuse, sexual promiscuity, overworking, or stealing from others?

5. Behind phobias?

6. Behind rescuing other people and trying to control their lives?

7. Behind confusion and helplessness?

8. Behind irrelevant behavior?

9. Behind super- reasonable, controlling behavior? 10. Behind self destructive, suicidal behavior?

You may be fooling only yourself if you are stuck in some of these patterns. Other people probably recognize your pain or at least see your behavior as the distortion that it is. The tragedy is that until you can see and be your real self, you consistently will alienate yourself from other people who love you and could support you as you work your way out of your pain.

When you are ready to go beyond your defensive walls to face and acknowledge your Hurt Inner Child, you must begin the process of developing a loving relationship with this shy, frightened part of yourself. Gaining its trust will take time and patience. After all, you have ignored it for years and the child within you may take some convincing that you are serious in your intention to honor its existence, its needs, and its feelings now. This stage calls for consistent effort on your part to tune into Your Inner Child, to imagine that you are holding this child close to your heart and embracing it in love and light.

Once your Inner Child begins to feel safe with you and to trust that you really are interested in its existence, it will begin to share with you what you may have forgotten and neglected to notice for years. You may experience deep feelings of anger, hurt, sadness, loneliness, despair or helplessness. If you are willing to allow your Inner Child to share these feelings with you, and if you are able to nurture yourself through these experiences of self-revelation, you will find yourself growing stronger and more whole with every step you take in this process of ever deepening self-acceptance and healing. The key is keeping yourself centered in the energy of unconditional love while managing to protect your Inner Child from other parts within you that may be intent upon sabotaging your progress, and robbing of your right to joy of living.

You get what you think you deserve and expect

Each of us contains a blueprint for the continual discovery of our true nature and purpose just like a bud grows damp under the earth. It pokes through weak mud, following the light, gently leaning toward nourishment. The sprout unfurls. With its flesh, it creates stalks, leaves, flowers and fruits. It flourishes through a growing season and withers with the frost. With each moment, the growth of this plant unfolds, following innate design. Our innate signature talents are the tools we can use to accomplish our life purpose. Part of us already knows the secret of our life blueprint but it remains unclear for most of us. However, if we allow our blueprint to unfold in its way, carefully encouraging its movements, time and nourishment, we will foster the development of an exceptional life.

What's Really Important to You?

At certain times in life, people take stock of where they are and where they want to go. Deciding what is important to us in our life's journey, including where we may be stuck, is the way to begin this life planning. The gift of knowing who you are and your life's work gives you the energy to transform your life.

You Get What You Tolerate

"I'll be happy when...." is the way many people are living their lives. Yet, happiness is not something that happens to you. Happiness is inside you now. You are motivated from within. You only have to allow happiness to surface.

Happiness = K (knowing who you are) times (X) D (discovering your life's work and purpose) X L (learning not to tolerate and ignore what's not important). Happiness (H) = K.D.L that's the formula for happiness--know yourself, your true calling and you get what you tolerate or what you do not tolerate.

Only when you know who you are (your signature talents, your values, assumptions/beliefs, guiding principles, vision and passions) are you able to bring your true self to your professional and personal lives. Your life signature is the tracing of the talents we are given and how we express them in our lives. Life is too short for doing work you don't enjoy.

Why not decide today, to live your life to its fullest?

Get a better life and regain your joie de vivre, dans la vie (in life).

Your Life can depend on how fast you can think

I will demonstrate to you the real life advantages of thinking, by telling you a story about the benefits of thinking fast and effectively, and how your LIFE can depend on how swift you think critically and right.

Sometimes in the distant past a rich man decided to go on a dangerous and adventurous safari. He took his favorite dog along for company. One day the dog started chasing butterflies and before long he discovered that he was lost. So, wandering about, he noticed a lion heading rapidly in his direction with the obvious intention of having him for dinner.

The dog started thinking: Oh my God, I'm in serious trouble! Then he noticed some bones on the ground next to him, and immediately settled down to chew on the bones with his back to the approaching wild animal.

Just as the lion was about to jump, the dog yelled loudly: god that was one delicious lion. I wonder if there are any more around here!

The lion stopped his attack in mid step and a look of terror came over him, and he disappeared into the bushes, after having heard the dog.

Meanwhile, a monkey who had been watching the whole scene from a nearby tree, realized he could put this knowledge to good use and trade it for protection from the lion. However, when the dog saw him heading after the lion with great speed, he figured that something must be up. The monkey soon caught up with the lion, told the lion the secrets, and negotiated a deal for himself with the lion.

When the dog saw the lion coming with the monkey on his back and he started thinking: what am I going to do now? But, instead of running, the dog sat down with his back to his attackers pretending he hasn't seen them yet. And just when they got close enough to hear, the dog said: Where's that stupid monkey. I just can't confide in him. I sent him off half an hour ago to bring me another lion, and he's still not back!"

What a brilliant way to think. This canine certainly knows his purpose. He is under no illusion as to what he is trying to *achieve-his survival is paramount and vital.* This blinding clarity helps him to think very quickly and cunningly in order to reach that goal. He is not getting nervous or dithering around thinking by wasting energy on questions such as: *What am I doing here?* Or *how did I get here?* or, to coin a current business trend, *what are my options?* There is one, and only one overriding thought-get *out of here, in one piece.*

Quick thinking is needed for survival-your survival. In fact, you might often feel like this unfortunate (or rather smart) dog when you go into certain meetings at work, or have exhausting discussions with highly charged loved ones determined to secure what they want. When you are clear about your purpose and goals in life, it makes it so much easier to think wisely and to your advantage.

But to be clear about your purpose is only the start. The dog in the story is very clear about his purpose-it is his survival. Like the dog, it is the way you *understand and give meaning* to your goal that will determine your success in achieving that purpose. The clever dog does not wonder about his immediate environment and whether he will survive it. He doesn't guess whether others will help him or get in the way and hinder him. Our cheeky dog could have understood several things about his situation: "the lion is stronger than me'" both the monkey and the lion will beat me: this situation is weighted too much against me or I'm lost -but if he had continued to read his situation in any of these ways he would not have survived. What made him achieve his purpose was his switch to, the strong, positive meaning he gave to his situation-and in doing so he was able to outwit the others.

Thinking quickly with a positive attitude is the only way to succeed in any situation. The story of the dog who thought he could survive by thinking positive; that he could escape death is a symbolic story that applies to all of us, human beings.

You can control your Mind and Body for success

Interaction with others affects everyone differently, but one feeling is common to everyone – nervousness. Palms begin sweating; feet start tapping, butterflies taking flight in your stomach, etc. There is a simple technique that you can use that will help you combat your nervousness.

It involves controlling your muscles and breathing in a little exercise that will relax you bodily and mentally. First, take a slow deep breath. You can be in any position, standing, sitting, or even lying down, so don't feel like you have to get into a certain position (it might appear odd to lie down on your back in the office while waiting to meet someone). Then contract your stomach muscles as though you are doing a sit-up. Then while keeping your muscles tightened or contracted, breathe out slowly. Just repeat this process until the nervousness has passed.

The muscle contractions will help prevent the introduction of chemical imbalances into your body that causes nervousness. The deep, slow breathing will help dispel any chemicals that have built up. The technique not only prepares your body physically, but will also focus your mind on the task at hand. As you focus on repeating the process, your concentration will take your thoughts off of what was causing you to be nervous and when you finish you will be able to focus on the issue and not yourself.

It is easy to blame others for your mistakes or shortcomings. If someone asks a question about something that you may be embarrassed about, don't immediately become negative and blame other people or situations. Accept responsibility for your actions and your past, but make sure that anything negative does not remain the focus. Turn negatives into positives.

Whatever you do, don't constantly shift the blame to others. It's okay to have had shortcomings in your past. The key in your interaction with others is to show how you've learned from those experiences and have moved on and overcome them.

Meeting and interacting with new people are often scary situations. It may feel as though your entire future rests in how you behave and perform during those first crucial 30 minutes to an hour. That level of tension can create lingering doubts and worry. It is critical that you not allow yourself to fall into that trap, but remain above it and stay confident. Think that no matter what happened, you will be fine, and that you will be able to handle it anyways; you did before, so this is just another time.

Think back over your past and try to remember all of your accomplishments. It may help to review your past and all of the highlights you've accomplished. Face it, you are a talented individual and are capable of anything, just like anyone else. If you can visualize success, then you are already halfway to your goal. You must remain confident in yourself, for if you can't be confident about yourself, who can? Your confidence begins with you. Practice it for a while, and you'll see how contagious it can be.

You've heard the expression, "GIGO - Garbage in, Garbage out". Only you can control what you think about. Focus on positive, optimistic thoughts and you will become positive and optimistic. Focus on thoughts of confidence, and you will become confident. Each of us becomes what we think about. A person will be judged by the way they appear.

You should try your best to maintain eye contact when interacting with others, especially when asking or answering any questions. Your eyes shouldn't wander around the room while you are talking. That makes people think you aren't telling the truth. If you have difficulty staring someone in the eyes, then stare at their nose, mouth, or another facial feature. They won't realize it and will think you are looking them in the eyes.

Remember that you can always become your own objective observer. Videotape yourself. By watching your own interaction with others, you can see what you did well and what needs extra work. It will allow you to focus your practice on areas that need the most improvement.

You can handle anything when you BELIEVE you can

You can handle anything when you accept the worst thing that can possibly happen in any situation. We all worry about the future and what MIGHT happen. We all want to know ahead of time what will happen in the future- tomorrow and beyond. But, predicting the future and what will happen with certainty and sureness is not possible. Therefore, the best thing to do in this case is to hope for the best, but we must accept the fact that the worst thing can happen also. Accepting the thought that the worst thing can happen, and that we can handle it, no matter how bad it might be, will give us peace of mind, because we internalize and accept the fact that we CAN handle it, and we believe that it is something we just cannot control, so, just accept it at its worst outcome possible. Fear of the unknown will disappear as soon as we realize that we can handle anything that comes our way. Consequently, we feel relaxed and more poised to dealing with the worst outcome. Once we accept that we can deal with and handle anything, and we start seeing the problem more logically, and usually we find solutions more suitable for any situation, because our brain works better when it is relaxed and not stressed or scared of the unknown.

Sometime, we will feel helpless and frustrated, because we cannot predict what will happen. To combat the feeling of being helpless, a self-defeating feeling, we must simply accept ourselves and the situation that seems to be overwhelming; realize that it is natural for anybody to feel anxious. We must not read into the future too much. And if we do, we must accept the worst possible outcome. We must believe that we can live with any result. Besides, life itself is limited, so why worry so much as if we are here on this earth forever. When we accept the fact that we can handle anything that might happen to us, including death itself, we become relaxed and happy, because what is there possibly that might be so bad since we already accepted the worst thing that might happen. You can conquer anything once you accept the worst scenario and possible outcome, because fear no longer controls us.

Change what you can- There is always hope and a better way of being to regain your joy of living Become Assertive not Aggressive

First of all, let us define what assertiveness is.

What is Assertiveness?

Assertiveness is the ability to express your feelings, opinions, beliefs, and needs directly, openly and honestly, while not violating the personal rights of others. Assertiveness does not in any way mean being *aggressive*. Aggressive behavior is self enhancing and self serving at the expense of others. It does not take other individuals' rights into consideration. Many People find it difficult to express their feelings honestly and openly because they lack assertiveness. This can become a problem when building a relationship, going out in the career world or communicating with friends, family members, and co-workers.

Psychologists differentiate between being "assertive" as distinguished from being "unassertive" (weak, passive, compliant, self-sacrificing) or "aggressive" (self-centered, inconsiderate, hostile, arrogantly demanding).

In general, assertiveness is representing yourself (your opinions, recommendations, etc) fully to others.

Assertiveness is a major aspect of self-leadership. Many experts would argue that you can't effectively lead others if you can't effectively lead yourself.

What Assertiveness is not:

Many people seem to confuse assertive behavior with aggression and hostility. Aggression is self-enhancing behavior at the expense of others. When acting aggressively, your classmates, friends and associates feelings are ignored, violated and not taken into consideration when interacting with them. Furthermore, and as a result of aggressive behavior, they feel hurt, humiliated, angry, and revengeful.

Negative effects of not being assertive

Many People find it difficult to express their feelings honestly and openly because they lack assertiveness. This can become a problem when building a relationship, going out in the career world or communicating with friends, family members, and co-workers.

What Will Assertiveness Do for You?

1- Develop your communication skills.

2- Allow you to feel self-confident.

3- Increase your self-esteem.

4- Help you to gain the respect of others.

5- Improve your decision-making ability.

How to Develop Assertive Skills

1- Be direct, honest, and open about your feelings, opinions and needs. State reasonable requests directly and firmly. State your goals or intentions in a direct and honest manner. State your point of view without being hesitant or apologetic. Being responsible for your own behavior will let you feel good about yourself.

2- Do not let your friends, classmates etc impose or reinforce their behaviors, values and ideas on you. Instead, let them know what you think, feel and want.

3- Be honest when giving and receiving compliments. Never put down a compliment and don't feel you must return one.

4- Learn to say no to unreasonable requests. Use the word "no" and offer an explanation if you choose to. Do not apologize and do not make up excuses. Paraphrase the other person's point of view. This will let him or her know that you hear and understand the request.

5- Avoid "why" questions. "Why" questions allows the listener to be defensive.

6- Recognize and respect the rights of your friends, and all others. For example if you are upset with them use "I" and "we" statements to express your feelings, instead of blaming and finger pointing "you" statements.

7- When communicating with others use an appropriate tone of voice and body posture. Maintain eye contact. Tone of voice should be appropriate to the situation. Stand or sit at a comfortable distance from the other person. Gestures can be used to emphasize what is being said and the word "I" and "we" should be used in statements to convey your feelings. For example, it is more appropriate to say "I am very disappointed that you didn't show up as planned", instead of saying: you are bad.

Train yourself to become assertive

Assertiveness training is an antidote to fear, shyness, passivity, and even anger, so there is an astonishingly wide range of situations in which this training is appropriate.

The following are actions you need to be able to do in the process of training yourself to become more assertive:

1- Speak up, make requests, ask for favors and generally insist that your rights be respected as a significant, equal human being.

2- Overcome the fears and self-depreciation that keep you from doing these things.

3- Express negative emotions (complaints, resentment, criticism, disagreement, intimidation, the desire to be left alone) and refuse requests when you want.

4- Show positive emotions (joy, pride, liking someone, attraction). Accept compliments with a simple "Thank you."

5- Ask why and question authority or tradition, not to rebel but to assume responsibility for asserting your share of control of the situation--and to make things better.

6- Initiate, carry on, change and terminate conversations comfortably. Share your feelings, opinions and experiences with others.

7- Deal with minor irritations before your anger builds into intense resentment and explosive aggression.

Steps you like to take:

Assertiveness:

Believe in your rights and realize where changes are needed

Many people recognize they are being taken advantage of and have difficulty saying "STOP". Others do not see themselves as unassertive, but do feel depressed or unfulfilled, have lots of physical ailments, have complaints about work but assume that others have the right to demand whatever they want. One may need to deal with the anxiety associated with changing, to reconcile the conflicts within your value system, to assess the repercussions of being assertive, and to prepare others for the changes they will see in your behavior or attitude. Talk to others about the appropriateness of being assertive in a specific situation that concerns you.

Value system origin:

Consider where your values (your "should have's") come from. Children are bombarded with rules: Don't be selfish, don't make mistakes, don't be emotional, don't tell people if you don't like them, don't be so unreasonable, don't question people, don't interrupt, don't trouble others with your problems, don't complain, don't upset others, don't brag, don't be anti-social, do what people ask you to do, help people who need help, and on and on. Do any of these instructions sound familiar? They help produce submissive children--and adults. There are probably good reasons for many of these rules-for-kids but as adults we need not blindly follow rules. Indeed, every one of these injunctions should be broken under certain conditions: You have a right to be first (sometimes), to make mistakes, to be emotional, to express your feelings, to have your own reasons, to stop others and ask questions, to ask for help, to ask for reasonable changes, to have your work acknowledged, to be alone, to say "no" or "I don't have time", and so on.

Besides recognizing that we have outgrown our unthinking submissiveness, we can further reduce our ambivalence about being assertive by recognizing the harm done by unassertiveness: (1) you cheat yourself and lose self-respect because you are dominated and can't change things, (2) you are forced to be dishonest, concealing your true feelings, (3) inequality and submissiveness threatens, if not destroys, love and respect, (4) a relationship based on your being a door mat, a slave, a "yes-person" a cute show piece or a source of income is oppressive and immoral, (5) since you must hide your true feeling, you may resort to subtle manipulation to get what you want and this creates resentment, and (6) your compliance rewards your oppressor. On the positive side, assertiveness leads to more self-respect and happiness. Build up your courage by reviewing all the reasons for changing.

Finally, there are obviously situations in which demanding immediate justice may not be wise: for example, if your assertive response will get you fired, or if it would cause an unwanted divorce, or if you might be assaulted, etc. Even in these more extreme cases, perhaps well planned or very gradual changes would be tolerated. Under any circumstances, discuss the reasons for becoming assertive with the other people involved so they will understand and approve (if possible) or at least respect you for being considerate of them, others, and yourself. Find appropriate ways of asserting yourself in each situation.

There are many ways to devise effective, tactful, fair assertive responses. Watch a good model. Discuss the problem situation with a spouse, a friend, a parent, a supervisor, a counselor or other persons. Carefully note how others respond to situations similar to yours and consider if they are being unassertive, assertive or aggressive. Read books about assertiveness. The following are steps to take in the process of becoming assertive:

Describe (to the other person involved) the troublesome situation as you see it. Be very specific about time and actions; don't make general accusations like "you're always hostile, upset, and busy". Be objective; don't suggest the other person is a total jerk. Focus on his/her behavior, not on his/her apparent motives.

Describe your feelings, using an "I" statement which shows you take responsibility for your feelings. Be firm and strong, look at them, be sure of yourself, and don't get emotional. Focus on positive feelings related to your goals if you can, not on your resentment of the other person. Sometimes it is helpful to explain why you feel as you do, so your statement becomes "I feel angry because you insulted me, for example.

Describe the changes you'd like made; be specific about what action should stop and what should start. Be sure the requested changes are reasonable, consider the other person's needs too, and be willing to make changes yourself in return. In some cases, you may already have explicit consequences in mind if the other person makes the desired changes and if he/she doesn't. If so, these should be described too. Don't make horrible and malevolent threats. This investment of time training yourself to become assertive will bring you joy of living, ultimately.

If I had my life to live over again

Staircase wit, or as the French call it "esprit d'escalier", is the surprising ability of our minds to come up with ALL those answers and rejoinders JUST as we start going up the stairs. When is too late for these new ideas to be implemented. The following are a few of those staircase wit ideas by someone who found out she was dying from cancer).

I would have gone to bed when I was sick instead of pretending the earth would go into a holding pattern if I weren't there for the day.

I would have burned the pink candle sculpted like a rose before it melted in storage.

I would have talked less and listened more.

I would have invited friends over to dinner even if the carpet was stained, or the sofa faded.

I would have eaten the popcorn in the living room and worried much less about the dirt when someone wanted to light a fire in the fireplace.

I would have taken the time to listen to my grandfather ramble about his youth.

I would have shared more of the responsibility carried by my husb9nd.

I would never have insisted the car windows be rolled up on a summer day because my hair had just been teased and sprayed.

I would have sat on the lawn with my grass stains.

I would have cried- and laughed less while watching television and more while watching life.

I would never have bought anything just because it was practical, wouldn't show sail, or was guaranteed to last a lifetime.

Instead of wishing away nine months of pregnancy, I'd have cherished every moment and realize that the wonderment growing inside me was the only chance in life to assist God in a miracle.

But mostly, given another shot at life, I would seize every minute, look at it and really see it. Live it and never give it back. And, STOP SWETING THE SMALL STUFF.

Don't worry about who doesn't like you, who has more, or who's doing what. Instead, let's cherish the relationships we have with those who do love us. Let's think about what-God HAS blessed us with, and what we are doing each day to promote ourselves mentally, physically, emotionally. I hope you have a blessed day. I hope you will enjoy every day as if it was your last day, and IT MIGHT JUST BE YOUR LAST DAY, since you really do not know when that day will be. Meanwhile, enjoy your relationships (at home with your family, at work/ business, and everywhere), and thus you will Regain control of Your Life and Be Happy Again.

Fight fair when you have to fight back

Sometimes you have to defend yourself against various people.

Try to fight fair even when the fighter tries to be totally unfair to you, because it is the right thing to do. No matter what happened during the fight do not lower yourself down to a lower level some attackers stoop to.

Try to rise above the jealous, the envious, the simply vicious, the vindictive, and the bad person who attacks you and your ego and character. You know that sometimes you have to return fire with fire…try to compromise because in any fight nobody wins, even if it seems that way.

Just keep going and do not let your attackers hurt you because if you do, you let them win twice: once when they attacked you and once more when they caused you to be hurt when you felt guilty or bad because of their attacks.

So just keep going and justice will prevail and you will be happy you did not let them hurt you.

Defend yourself when you really have to. But, do not retaliate simply for the sake of retaliating; for the sake of

TEACHING "someone" a lesson, because this will only create a vicious circle of action-reaction (people hurt you and you hurt them back vindictively- in retaliation- and a result they find another way to hurt you back in reaction, and the circle continues. Defend yourself only to stop unjust ice done against you if it is really worth something or just let it go; the offender will pay for his or her bad deed some other time. Some people like to retaliate and "pay back", as they say, their perceived offenders. Don't retaliate, because you will "pay", literally, with something (anger, rage, anxiety, stress, etc). However, when you simply forgive and not retaliate you regain your joy of living and you put the past behind you and move ahead in your life.

Make your Relationships work

Life is never perfect at work, school, home, or wherever. You will always have challenges and real problems to deal with. It has been said actually that the difference between successful people and failures is the ability of the successful people to face problems (challenges), deal and solve them, as opposed to failures who usually when faced with a challenge they ignore the problem hoping it will go away or just burry their heads in the sand, so to speak.

Becoming successful requires us to do the following:

Isolating (identifying) the problem is the first step in solving a relationship problem or any type of problem, as a matter of fact.

The real problem must be pinpointed, otherwise the wrong solution will be found.

Method #1: Listen for themes behind the statements. Learn to recognize the themes that come up more frequently between you two. Is it anger, money, sex, apathy, anxiety, lack of trust, lack of respect, etc?

Method #2: To ensure objectivity from being emotionally involved, write down your version of the problem. Be specific. Give evidence for each statement you make.

1. Start with a small problem and both learn the systematic way of arriving at a solution.

2. Establish rapport (open approach between you and your partner) with each other.

3. Reduce hostility by:

   1- Indirect release (inside a car by yourself, for example, insult spouse)

   2- Ask why you are feeling so angry and find out - will reduce anger.

   3- Reorient a person's attitude toward problem solving.

Positive homework assignments

1- Make a written list of things you and your spouse/ partner have in common.

2- Make a list of whatever your spouse/partner does well.

3- Role switching to see things from the other person's view.

4- Record the fights and arguments and then list them when you're quiet to analyze problems.

Now is the time to Face the problem, and solve it; then, be happy that you did, and move to the next level in your life. Enjoy your relationship; don't suffer and just endure it as if it is a condemnation and life sentence. Realize that for any problem there is a corresponding solution and it your job and responsibility to find the suitable solution, and put into ACTION swiftly and quickly. It is possible that your partner might help solve the problem at hand, but why not TAKE the LEAD and take the initiative by taking ACTION. Take action and if it turns out to be the wrong one, then just correct it and move on to the next action. When you take responsibility by taking action you will You can Regain control of Your Life and Be Happy Again.

Take complete charge of your life

No human is perfect, and you are a human; therefore, you are not perfect, and you cannot be perfect. The sooner you accept that fact and truth that you are in complete charge of your life and you are responsible for all aspects of your life, the sooner you will be happy. Assume and take full responsibility for your life, and do not blame your parents if you did not get a good education or anything you might think that your parents were supposed to provide you with. You can blame your parents as long as you want, but blaming them will never get you that education or anything else missing, so, take charge now and start right now doing what you need to do to get what you need and want, and stop blaming your parents by putting a closure on the past, do it right now because it is the only right thing to do to empower you with a new powers you did not have before.

Whatever your age is, it is time to stop blaming others and now is the time to take full charge of your life, your education, your finances, your health, your social life, and all the other aspects of your life. Assume responsibility and have the power over your life, do not give it to anybody else. Joy of living comes from feeling and being empowered, in charge, and in control of one's life, not by feeling helpless, giving up and relinquishing your right of taking charge of your life and taking care of yourself. Don't serve time, let time serve you; enjoy life while are alive.

Chapter # 5 — Control Your Behavior not your Emotions

SUCH AS Anger

Manage your anger or it will kill you

Under certain circumstances, profanity provides a relief denied even to prayer.

Mark Twain

Anger can be a physiological and or psychological response to a perceived threat to one's self or important others present, past, or future. The threat may seem to be real, discussed, or imagined. Anger is often a response to the perception of threat due to a physical conflict, injustice, negligence, humiliation or betrayal among other contentions. The expression of anger can be through active or passive behaviors. In the case of "active" emotion the angry person "lashes out" verbally or physically at an intended target. When anger is a "passive" emotion it is characterized by silent sulking, passive-aggressive behavior (hostility) and tension. Humans often experience anger empathetically: for example, after reading an article about a minority experiencing racism, one may experience anger, even though she/he is not the actual victim. Anger is usually magnified and extended in time when a cognitive decision is made about the intent of the individual (or organization or object) interpreted as inflicting the pain. In other words, if one decides the pain infliction was intentional, "deliberate," the emotion is usually more intense.

The Roots of Your Anger

You can manage anger to regain your joy in life. Your education about anger began when you were a toddler. As soon as you were able to crawl and explore your big, fascinating world, you began to assert your individuality and separateness from your parents. In the process, you encountered lots of "nos and don'ts". Powerful angry feelings rose inside you when you were frustrated in your explorations. Probably you expressed yourself in no uncertain terms with loud, angry tears, a red face, and maybe even kicking, fighting arms and legs. Your parents were interfering with your freedom. The world no longer seemed to revolve around you, so that your wants and needs were fulfilled without question. You protested angrily. The manner in which your parents reacted to your rage was crucial to your development. If they were friendly with their own anger and able to experience and express it appropriately, they were not alarmed when they saw your anger emerge. They acknowledged your feelings without fear and began the process of teaching you to handle these powerful feelings in appropriate, constructive ways. "I understand that you are angry. It's OK to be angry, but it's not OK to hit me when you're angry. It's OK to be angry, but you may not disrupt dinner. I'm going to put you in your room where you'll be safe until you're finished being angry.

Your parents' attitudes about anger are the key to what you learned about this emotion when you were a child. If you felt and sensed your parents' calm acceptance of your angry feelings, you gradually learned to accept them without fear too. Eventually you learned to handle these powerful feelings constructively. But if your parents were afraid of anger themselves, you felt and sensed their fear when you became angry. You learned to associate fear with the experience of anger.

If your parents expressed their fear by becoming angry too, escalating their feelings over yours in a threatening, overpowering way, you became frightened of anger. You taught yourself to hide your rage from your parents so you wouldn't upset them. If this pattern was not interrupted or changed, you didn't progress beyond this level of development to master your anger .Instead you became more and more adept at stuffing your feelings inside yourself. You probably had periodic temper tantrums when you became really overloaded with repressed feelings and something provoked your buried rage. But these episodes also set off your parents' fears and reinforced your learning that anger is a bad, destructive monster to be avoided no matter what the cost to you.

If your parents were fearful, helpless, and ineffective in their efforts to cope with your anger, you learned that you could manipulate them with your rage. If this was *your* experience, you discovered power in your anger in a way that was destructive for you. You learned that you could get your way by using your anger as a weapon to frighten your parents and get them to accommodate to what you wanted. You became inappropriately powerful, holding the threat of an angry outburst over your parents' heads. They in turn tried to keep you happy and appeased to avoid your rages. Either way, you got stuck in your developmental process. Rather than learning to master your anger through facing your feelings and learning to handle them in constructive, appropriate ways, you learned instead to fear the anger monster and hide it, or to use it to frighten others into doing what you wanted.

Your anger remained like an untrained family dog that is kept fenced in the backyard. The dog is too undisciplined to be an enjoyable playmate for family members. If he accidentally gets into the house, he races about in his unbounded excitement, jumping on people and creating chaos and confusion as soon as he can be caught, he is banished again to his backyard domain. He remains a lonely beast, isolated and confined, away- from the warmth and love of his master's touch, discipline, and teaching. Unless the family decides to train him, love him, and make him a part of their lives, he is doomed to being a monster, nuisance dog, a problem to everyone he encounters.

If you didn't begin to learn as a child to master your anger, you may have had some serious problems by the time your teenage years rolled around. Anger repressors who have periodic temper outburst may turn to drugs and alcohol, sexual acting out, failure in school, compulsive perfectionist behavior, overeating, overachieving, depression, or even suicide. Pouting, passive refusal to act, and physical symptoms like stomachaches, headaches hyperactivity, and allergies are common. Anger abusers also may turn to illegal activities, seeking to discover where the limits of their power lie. Your parents (and other parenting figures like teachers, coaches, other kids' parents, and radio. and television) were your anger teachers. You progressed in your learning about anger as far as they had progressed in theirs, unless you have taken responsibility as an adult for *reeducating yourself about this powerful and important emotion.*

Mastering anger is a challenge you can meet no matter what age you are when you decide to grow beyond your fears and into the fullness of your personal power and potential for health, happiness, and success.

Anger is like poison, if you do not control it; it will kill you slowly. So, let anger go and replace it with compassion, love, and forgiveness for all people and most importantly for yourself: Love and forgive yourself; remember to forgive others and enjoy life not endure it.

Replace Anger with love

Replace anger with love, love all people, or at least feel sorry for them if they are acting unjustly against you. Do not keep anger, under any circumstances inside you to eat you up. It has been said that: getting angry is like taking a small dose of some-slow-acting poison everyday of your life.

Don't be a hero by getting even with people who treated you unjustly; just forgive them, be the BIG person, and let it go; you will have joy of living not feeling of being poisoned and victimized. You will feel much better about yourself when you forgive others their mistakes and transgressions; they are humans after all, so just forgive and do not worry about them repeating their mistakes, because that is their problem, and not yours if they repeat the same mistake over and over again.

Most people feel as follows:

1) When a loss threatens, they feel anxious.

2) When a loss occurs, they feel hurt.

3) When hurt is held back, it creates anger.

4) When anger is held back, it creates guilt.

5) When guilt is unrelieved, it creates depression.

6) If you take care of your fear, hurt, and anger, the guilt and depression will take care of themselves.

7) Fear is the threat of loss or an injury. It may be a real loss or just imaginary.

8) Knowing what you are afraid of will make your fear easier to manage.

9) To take risks successfully, you must become aware of and familiar with your own experience of fear. Just like a driver speeding; speeding causes threat of injury (fear), but if a driver anticipated that; then he would have managed it properly.

10) Coping with fear: imagine the worst outcome and accept it, then try to improve on it.

In summary, if you accept losses as part of life and realize that you can handle any loss no matter how small or big the loss might be; including the loss of life itself, then you would not feel any strong feeling of being hurt. And if you do not hold back feeling of being hurt you would not feel angry. You must accept that anger is also part of life and let it (anger) go. Letting anger get the best of us (consume us) can be very damaging to us. Accept your anger and realize that the world might not be fair, but don't make it double trouble by dwelling on how unjust is the world to us; just accept it as part of living and let it go. If you hold anger and let it boil inside you, it will make you feel so bad such that you will not do anything to fix and rectify the INJUSTICE. This feeling of anger becomes feeling of guilt, which will become depression.

Be smart and accept unjust acts against you as part of life and living in general, and do not feel as a victim; just do something if you can or just accept (if you cannot change anything) the situation as a loss which is part of life and move on with your endeavor of living good life. And, do not forget to let go of anger, and create love by loving all others even if they make you angry; you will feel better and healthier. Anger is the symptom of fear. Handle your anger intelligently and you will resolve your anger issues, no matter what they are.

Just be yourself, and you will be happy

The most important risk you can take is to be honest in expressing your feelings freely, and being yourself with your dual sides (good and bad sides). If you do not express what you feel, you are forced to use defenses to keep unwanted feeling hidden away.

A defense is built into your character and inherent in everyone's personality. Defenses rob you of your energy and transform you into a person who does only what he or she thinks is acceptable by others (conforming to others' standards) because he or she feels uncomfortable being himself or herself; since being oneself might engender resentment by others who disagree. For example, peer pressure is due to people's belief that they must succumb and conform to what others expect of them, and not do what they want. This is in accordance with the myth that says "to get along you must go along". In the process of conforming to others, sometimes, people commit unlawful acts, such as when a teenager accepts to try drugs because his or her peers put pressure on them. The best way of living life to its fullest is by accepting yourself with your faults (you are a human, and by default you cannot be perfect), and realize that others will disagree with you, and they will pressure you into doing things you do not want to do. Be yourself; stand for your convictions and principles strongly, because if you do not stand for something, you will fall for anything, as the adage has it.

Control your Anger, Before It Controls You

We all know what anger is, and we've all felt it: whether as a fleeting annoyance or as full-fledged rage. Anger is a completely normal, usually healthy, human emotion. But when it gets out of control and turns destructive, it can lead to problems—problems at work, in your personal relationships, and in the overall quality of your life. And it can make you feel as though you're at the mercy of an unpredictable and powerful emotion.

What is Anger?

Anger is "an emotional state that varies in intensity from mild irritation to intense fury and rage," according to Charles Spielberger, PhD, a psychologist who specializes in the study of anger. Like other emotions, it is accompanied by physiological and biological changes; when you get angry, your heart rate and blood pressure go up, as do the levels of your energy hormones, adrenaline, and noradrenalin.

Anger can be caused by both external and internal events. You could be angry at a specific person (Such as a coworker or supervisor) or event (a traffic jam, a canceled flight), or your anger could be caused by worrying or brooding about your personal problems. Memories of traumatic or enraging events can also trigger angry feelings.

Expressing Anger:

The instinctive, natural way to express anger is to respond aggressively. Anger is a natural, adaptive response to threats; it inspires powerful, often aggressive, feelings and behaviors, which allow us to fight and to defend ourselves when we are attacked. A certain amount of anger, therefore, is necessary to our survival.

On the other hand, we can't physically lash out at every person or object that annoys us. Laws, social norms, and common sense place limits on how far our anger can take us.

People use a variety of both conscious and unconscious processes to deal with their angry feelings. <u>The three main approaches are expressing, suppressing, and calming:</u>

1- Expressing your angry feelings in an assertive—not aggressive—manner is the healthiest way to express anger. To do this, you have to learn how to make clear what your needs are, and how to get them met, without hurting others. Being assertive doesn't mean being pushy or demanding; it means being respectful of yourself and others.

2- Suppressing anger can be dangerous. This happens when you hold in your anger, stop thinking about it, and focus on something positive. The aim is to inhibit or suppress your anger and convert it into more constructive behavior. The danger in this type of response is that if it isn't allowed outward expression, your anger can turn inward—on yourself. Anger turned inward may cause hypertension, high blood pressure, or depression.

Unexpressed anger can create other problems. *It can lead to pathological expressions of anger, such as passive-aggressive behavior (getting back at people indirectly, without telling them why, rather than confronting them head-on) or a personality that seems perpetually cynical and hostile. People who are constantly putting others down, criticizing everything, and making cynical comments haven't learned how to constructively express their anger.* Not surprisingly, these kinds of people aren't likely to have many successful relationships.

3- Calming anger down inside. This means not just controlling your outward behavior, but also controlling your internal responses, taking steps to lower your heart rate, calm yourself down, let the feelings subside, let go, put a closure and have peace of mind.

You can Control Your Anger

Life does not always go smoothly. Every day you face situations where your self-control will be challenged. Feelings of frustration and stress become outbursts of anger, wreaking havoc throughout your life. Does this sound like you or someone you know?

1. Do you wish you had more control over your emotions in stressful situations?

2. Do you often regret your actions when you lose your temper and wish you had handled the situation differently?

3. Do co-workers and superiors view your anger as unprofessional?

4. Are angry outbursts and confrontations straining your relationship with your family?

5. Have you been told by a friend or a legal institution that you need anger management?

Would you rather control your anger or be free of it?

When you perceive you are about to lose control, simply ask yourself the easy-to-learn and easy-to-remember questions: is there anything worth losing your health for?

The answer, obviously, is NO. Immediately, you will feel the tightness leaving your stomach, shoulders and chest. In its place, you will feel ease, relaxation and confidence. You will no longer feel angry and out of control, stressed and frustrated. Feeling more relaxed, you will be capable of handling whatever life throws at you more easily. The noise of your mind will subside, and you will have the clarity of mind to say and do what is appropriate and natural in order to master any life situation.

You don't have to struggle with anger management anymore.

What would your life be like if you were free of anger? Take a brief moment right now and think about what that would feel like? Imagine that from this moment forward, you experience nothing but joy and calm in any given situation at least 90 percent of the time for the rest of your life.

You may be saying "You don't know my problems. My life sucks." Or, "That's just life. I've always felt this way and I probably always will." But that's not how it has to be.

If you are not having the experience of happiness and fun in any situation, then you may be holding feelings that do not allow you to experience your own natural sense of well-being. In other words, *if you do not feel as happy, confident and positive as you desire, it is for one simple reason: you are literally holding feelings that actually prevent you from experiencing joy.*

Cheer up, the good news is here:

The good news is that the feelings you have are just feelings. They are not you and they are not facts. You can let these feelings go just as easily as you can let an object you are holding drop to the ground. These feelings you hold will only prevent you from having exactly what you want for as long as you hold them. Whether you choose to hold them for the rest of your life or whether you choose to release them right now—the decision is yours.

Would I rather be angry? Or would I rather be happy?

I rather be happy than angry, of course.

You can choose to manage anger as follows:

1. The first step towards managing anger in our personal relationships appropriately is the identification of the mistaken attitudes and convictions that predispose us to being excessively angry in the first place!

2. Once these mistakes have been corrected, we will be less likely to fly off the handle than we were. The second step is the identification of those factors from our

childhood that prevents us from expressing our anger as appropriately as we otherwise might. These factors include fear, denial, ignorance, and so on.

These impediments to the effective and appropriate management of our anger towards others can be removed so that our suppressed anger will NOT compound itself inside of us as it has been doing for years in the past.

3. The third step is learning the appropriate modes of expressing our "legitimate" anger at others so that we can begin to cope more effectively with anger provoking situations as they arise in our personal relationships. When we are anxious or depressed in our relationships, we are often experiencing the consequences of our suppressed anger. The problem is that we have suppressed our anger so deeply that we succeeded in concealing it from our own selves! All we are left with is the residual evidence of it, our anxiety or our depression. When we are depressed, very often we are also angry at our self without realizing it.

Learning to appropriately manage our anger at ourselves is the antidote to much of alcoholism and drug abuse. But the management of our anger does not end in learning these new and more appropriate ways to express it. There remains one last step.

4. The fourth step in the Anger Management process is to bind up the wounds that may have been left by the potentially devastating emotional impact of anger. "Anger wounds" left in us against those who have wronged us. If we do not complete this mopping and cleansing up step, we will cling to the resentment of having been done wrong and will carry the festering and rotten residue of our anger and rage in our hearts forever.

One of the most effective means of giving ourselves immediate relief from anger in our personal relationships is to forgive others.

Many of us cannot forgive those who have trespassed against us.

Something below the level of our conscious awareness prevents us from relieving our residual anger by forgiving the other person and we then carry a grudge in our hearts for a long miserable time. This unresolved anger poisons our relationship with our friends and loved ones. It even spoils our relationship with ourselves! We make our own lives mean and miserable instead of happy and full. Very often the feeling is, "Why should I forgive them? What they did was WRONG" But, is forgiveness for those who only do us right? Most people have a hard time forgiving others simply because they have a wrong understanding of what forgiveness is! When you forgive someone, it does not mean that you condone or are legitimizing their behavior toward you. To forgive them means that you refuse to carry painful and debilitating grudges around with you for the rest of your life! You are "refusing" to cling to the resentment of them having done you wrong. You are giving yourself some immediate relief from your OWN anger!

To forgive, then, is an act that we do on our OWN behalf.

It has nothing to do with "lifting" the other person's sin! You are not doing it for their sake. You are doing it for yourself. This is a choice you are making on your OWN terms in order to relieve your OWN unexpressed and hurtful emotions of anger.

Anger Management

The goal of anger management is to reduce both your emotional feelings and the physiological arousal that anger causes. You can't get rid of, or avoid, the things or the people that enrage you, nor can you change them, but you can learn to control your reactions.

Are You Too Angry?

Chances are good that if you do have a problem with anger, you already know it. If you find yourself acting in ways that seem out of control and frightening, you need help finding better ways to deal with this emotion.

Why Are Some People More Angrier than Others?

According to Jerry Deffenbacher, PhD, a psychologist who specializes in anger management, some people really are more "hotheaded" than others are; they get angry more easily and more intensely than the average person does. There are also those who don't show their anger in loud spectacular ways but are chronically irritable and grumpy. Easily angered people don't always curse and throw things; sometimes they withdraw socially, sulk, or get physically ill.

People who are easily angered generally have what some psychologists call a low tolerance for frustration, meaning simply that they feel that they should not have to be subjected to frustration, inconvenience, or annoyance. They can't take things in stride, and they're particularly infuriated if the situation seems somehow unjust: for example, being corrected for a minor mistake.

What makes these people this way? Many things: One cause may be genetic or physiological: There is evidence that some children are born irritable, touchy, and easily angered, and that these signs are present from a very early age. Another may be sociocultural. Anger is often regarded as negative; we're taught that it's all right to express anxiety, depression, or other emotions but not to express anger. As a result, we don't learn how to handle it or channel it constructively.

Is It Good to "Let it All Out?"

Psychologists now say that this is a dangerous myth. Some people use this theory as a license to hurt others. Research has found that "letting it rip" with anger actually escalates anger and aggression and does nothing to help you (or the person you're angry with) resolve the situation.

It's best to find out what it is that triggers your anger, and then to develop strategies to keep those triggers from tipping you over the edge.

Relaxation as a way to deal with anger

Simple relaxation tools, such as deep breathing and relaxing imagery, can help calm down angry feelings. There are books and courses that can teach you relaxation techniques, and once you learn the techniques, you can call upon them in any situation. If you are involved in a relationship where both partners are hot-tempered, it might be a good idea for both of you to learn these techniques.

Some simple steps you can try:

- Breathe deeply, from your diaphragm; breathing from your chest won't relax you. Picture your breath coming up from your "gut."

- Slowly repeat a calm word or phrase such as "relax," "take it easy." "love," Repeat it to yourself while breathing deeply.

- Use imagery; visualize a relaxing experience, from either your memory or your imagination.

- Non strenuous, slow yoga-like exercises can relax your muscles and make you feel much calmer. Learn to use them automatically when you're in a tense situation.

Dealing with anger using cognitive restructuring (the way you think)

Simply put, this means changing the way you think. Angry people tend to curse, swear, or speak in highly colorful terms that reflect their inner thoughts. When you're angry, your thinking can get very exaggerated and overly dramatic. Try replacing these thoughts with more rational ones. For instance, instead of telling yourself, "oh, it's awful, it's terrible, everything's ruined," tell yourself, "it's frustrating, and it's understandable that I'm upset about it, but it's not the end of the world and getting angry is not going to fix it anyhow."

Be careful of words like "never" or "always" when talking about yourself or someone else. Do not say things like: "you're always forgetting things" because they are not just inaccurate, they also serve to make you feel that your anger is justified and that there's no way to solve the problem. They also alienate and humiliate people who might otherwise be willing to work with you on a solution.

Remind yourself that getting angry is not going to fix anything that it won't make you feel better (and may actually make you feel worse).

Logic defeats anger, because anger, even when it's justified, can quickly become irrational. So use cold hard logic on yourself. *Remind yourself that the world is "not out to get you,"* you're just experiencing some rough spots of daily life. Do this each time you feel anger getting the best of you, and it'll help you get a more balanced perspective. *Angry people tend to demand things: fairness, appreciation, agreement, willingness to do things their way.* Everyone wants these things, and we are all hurt and disappointed when we don't get them, but angry people demand them, and when their demands aren't met, their disappointment becomes anger. As part of their cognitive restructuring, angry people need to become aware of their demanding nature and translate their expectations into desires. In other words, saying, "I would like" something is healthier than saying, "I demand" or "I must have" something. When you're unable to get what you want, you will experience the normal reactions—frustration, disappointment, hurt—but not anger. Some angry people use this anger as a way to avoid feeling hurt, but that doesn't mean the hurt goes away.

Problem Solving: Not every problem has a desirable solution

Sometimes, our anger and frustration are caused by very real and inescapable problems in our lives. Not all anger is misplaced, and often it's a healthy, natural response to these difficulties. There is also a cultural belief that every problem has a solution, and it adds to our frustration to find out that this isn't always the case. *The best attitude to bring to such a situation, then, is not to focus on finding the solution, but rather on how you handle and face the problem.*

Make a plan, and check your progress along the way. Resolve to give it your best, but also not to punish yourself if an answer doesn't come right away. If you can approach it with your best intentions and efforts and make a serious attempt to face it head-on, you will be less likely to lose patience and fall into all-or-nothing thinking, even if the problem does not get solved right away.

Better Communication

Angry people tend to jump to conclusions and act on them, and unfortunately some of those conclusions can be very inaccurate. The first thing to do if you're in a heated discussion is slow down and think through your responses. Don't say the first thing that comes into your head, but slow down and think carefully about what you want to say. At the same time, listen carefully to what the other person is saying and take your time before answering. Listen, too, to what is underlying the anger.

For instance, if you like a certain amount of freedom and personal space, and your "significant other" wants more connection and closeness. If he or she starts complaining about your activities, don't retaliate by painting your partner as a jailer, a warden, or an albatross (shackle) around your neck.

It's natural to get defensive when you're criticized, but don't fight back. Instead, listen to what's underlying the words: the message that this person might feel neglected and unloved. It may take a lot of patient questioning on your part, and it may require some breathing space, but don't let your anger—or a partner's—let a discussion spin out of control. Keeping your cool can keep the situation from becoming a disastrous one.

Using Humor

"Silly humor" can help defuse rage in a number of ways. For one thing, it can help you get a more balanced perspective. When you get angry and call someone a name or refer to them in some imaginative phrase, stop and picture what that word would literally look like. If you're at work and you think of a coworker as a "dirt bag" or a "single-cell life form," for example, picture a large bag full of dirt sitting at your colleague's desk, talking on the phone, going to meetings. Do this whenever a name comes into your head about another person. If you can, draw a picture of what the actual thing might look like. This will take a lot of the edge off your fury; and humor can always be relied on to help unknot a tense situation.

The underlying message of highly angry people, Dr. Deffenbacher says, is "things must go my way!" Angry people tend to feel that they are morally right, that any blocking or changing of their plans is an unbearable indignity and that they should NOT have to suffer this way. Maybe other people do, but not them!

When you feel that urge, he suggests, picture yourself as a god or goddess, a supreme ruler, who owns the streets and stores and office space, striding alone and having your way in all situations while others defer to you. The more detail you can get into your imaginary scenes, the more chances you have to realize that maybe you are being unreasonable; you'll also realize how unimportant the things you're angry about really are. There are two cautions in using humor. First, don't try to just "laugh off" your problems; rather, use humor to help yourself face them more constructively. Second, don't give in to harsh, sarcastic humor; that's just another form of unhealthy anger expression.

What these techniques have in common is a refusal to take yourself too seriously. Anger is a serious emotion, but it's often accompanied by ideas that, if examined, can make you laugh.

Changing Your Environment

Sometimes it's our immediate surroundings that give us cause for irritation and fury. Problems and responsibilities can weigh on you and make you feel angry at the "trap" you seem to have fallen into and all the people and things that form that trap.

Give yourself a break. Make sure you have some "personal time" scheduled for times of the day that you know are particularly stressful.

Tips for taking it easy on yourself when angry

Timing: If you and your spouse tend to fight when you discuss things at night—perhaps you're tired, or distracted, or maybe it's just habit—try changing the times when you talk about important matters so these talks don't turn into arguments.

Avoidance: If your child's chaotic room makes you furious every time you walk by it, shut the door. Don't make yourself look at what infuriates you. Don't say, "well, my child should clean up the room so I won't have to be angry!" That's not the point. The point is to keep yourself calm.

Finding alternatives: If your daily commute through traffic leaves you in a state of rage and frustration, give yourself a project—learn or map out a different route, one that's less congested or more scenic. Or find another alternative, such as a bus or commuter train.

Do You Need Counseling to deal with your anger?

If you feel that your anger is really out of control, if it is having an impact on your relationships and on important parts of your life, you might consider counseling to learn how to handle it better. A psychologist or other licensed mental health professional can work with you in developing a range of techniques for changing your thinking and your behavior.

When you talk to a prospective therapist, tell her or him that you have problems with anger that you want to work on, and ask about his or her approach to anger management. Make sure this isn't only a course of action designed to "put you in touch with your feelings and express them"—that may be precisely what your problem is. With counseling, psychologists say, a highly angry person can move closer to a middle range of anger in about 8 to 10 weeks, depending on the circumstances and the techniques used.

What About Assertiveness Training?

It's true that angry people need to learn to become assertive (rather than aggressive), but most books and courses on developing assertiveness are aimed at people who don't feel enough anger. These people are more passive and acquiescent than the average person; they tend to let others walk all over them. That isn't something that most angry people do. Still, these books can contain some useful tactics to use in frustrating situations.

Remember, you can't eliminate anger—and it wouldn't be a good idea if you could. In spite of all your efforts, things will happen that will cause you anger; and sometimes it will be justifiable anger. Life will be filled with frustration, pain, loss, and the unpredictable actions of others. You can't change that; but you can change the way you let such events affect you. Controlling your angry responses can keep them from making you even unhappier in the long run.

You can handle your Anger before it becomes rage

Anger is a destructive emotion if it is not controlled and handled properly. The following are a few points for managing anger before it becomes rage:

1. Accept your anger as a natural response, because if you see your anger as a bad and unjust emotion you only multiply your anger to the point of rage and explosion.

2. Let your anger out. Don't bottle your anger indefinitely. Talk about your anger calmly and rationally. Talk about irritations before they become rage/anger with the concerned party such as your spouse.

3. Forgive other people who made you angry and forgive yourself when you lose your temper.

The key to managing anger is in letting out and venting it and not in bottling it inside.

If you find yourself bottling anger it may be because of the following reasons:

1. You think you should be nice all the time. You believe that losing your temper will make people dislike you.

2. You think you have to protect others by holding your anger because you assume that others will not be able to handle your anger.

Admitting your anger and hurt empowers you

Real strength is being able to admit one's weaknesses honestly, to say that one is hurt and afraid, and still take a forceful stand and carry on. Real strength comes from accepting your vulnerability and weaknesses as a human being.

For example, anger is an emotion that generates and engenders the feeling of being hurt, especially if we do not resolve the problem and the cause of our anger and its effects (our feeling of being hurt).

To risk expressing anger is the road to happiness and empowerment.

Here is how:

1) Expressing anger - to tell the person who hurt you that he did so. Do it simply and directly and state that you feel angry. Then wait for his or her response.

2) If a person does not love you because you get angry when he hurts you, he did not love you before.

3) If you are afraid of losing control by getting angry and therefore hold it in, you are only setting yourself up for the day when you cannot hold it in anymore.

4) What is a relationship worth in which you cannot express yourself (what and how you feel)?

5) You have to risk being true to your feelings or you can never be true to yourself.

6) Anger is the natural result of being hurt, injured, let down, disappointed, tricked, made a fool of, taken advantage of, used, insulted, ridiculed.

7) If you hold anger in all the time, it can destroy you.

So, why don't you just be yourself, and worry no more about Jane and Joe (what others think). You will be happy, successful, when you stop trying to be someone else. Just be yourself. Anger when expressed in a civilized manner leads to peace of mind.

Anger's final solution: Forgive all people forever

Vidura said: There is one only defect in forgiving persons and not another; that defect is that people take a forgiving person to be weak. That defect, however, should not be taken into consideration, for forgiveness is a great power. Forgiveness is a virtue of the weak, and an ornament of the strong. Forgiveness subdues (all) in this world; what is there that forgiveness cannot achieve? What can a wicked person do unto him who carries the sabre of forgiveness in his hand? Fire falling on the grassless ground is extinguished of itself. And unforgiving individual defiles himself with many enormities. Righteousness is the one highest good; and forgiveness is the one supreme peace; knowledge is one supreme contentment; and benevolence, one sole happiness.

Visualize and picture the jam-packed screen in front of a stressed air traffic controller. Picture the disorder in the room and the disarray of planes on the screen. Now imagine that your unresolved grievances are the planes on that screen that have been circling for days and weeks. Most of the other planes have landed, but your unresolved grievances continue to take up precious air space, draining resources that may be needed in an emergency. Having them on the screen forces you to work harder and increases the chance for accidents. The grievance planes become a source of stress and burnout is often the result.

HOW DID YOU GET ANGRY AND POSSIBLY OUTRAGED IN THE FIRST PLACE?

You took something too personally.

You continued to blame the person who hurt you for how bad you felt.

You created a grievance story which you made yourself believe in, even though it is probably not true, but you made all kinds of assumptions which led you to the wrong conclusion. You can UNDO your belief in this "VICTIM" story, and become powerful instead of powerless.

WHAT IS FORGIVENESS?

Forgiveness is the mental, emotional and/or spiritual process of ceasing to feel resentment, indignation or anger against another person for a perceived offence, difference or mistake, or ceasing to demand punishment or restitution.

Most world religions include teachings on the nature of forgiveness, and many of these teachings provide an underlying basis for many varying modern day traditions and practices of forgiveness. However, throughout the ages, philosophers have studied forgiveness apart from religion. In addition, as in other areas of human inquiry, science is beginning to question religious concepts of forgiveness. Psychology, sociology and medicine are among the scientific disciplines researching forgiveness or aspects of forgiveness.

Instances of teachings on forgiveness such as the parable of the Prodigal Son and Mahatma Gandhi's forgiveness of his assassin as he lay dying are well known instances of such teachings and practices of forgiveness. Some religious doctrines or philosophies place greater emphasis on the need for humans to find some sort of divine forgiveness for their own shortcomings, others place greater emphasis on the need for humans to practice forgiveness between one another, yet others make little or no distinction between human and/or divine forgiveness.

. Forgiveness is the peace you learn to feel when you allow these airplanes (FEELINGS OF ANGER) land and disappear from your radar screen (your feelings of anger leaving you in peace).

. Forgiveness is for you and not the offender.

. Forgiveness is taking back your power.

. Forgiveness is taking responsibility for how you feel.

. Forgiveness is about your healing and not about the people who hurt you.

. Forgiveness is a trainable skill just like learning to paint.

. Forgiveness helps you get control over sour feelings.

. Forgiveness can improve your mental and physical health.

. Forgiveness is becoming a hero instead of a victim.

. Forgiveness is a choice.

. Everyone can learn to forgive.

The Art of Negotiations for Success and joy of living

People engage in negotiating with each other every day. Negotiation is part of living, and it can lead to a happy or a miserable life, depending on your negotiating skills.

Negotiation ranges from small matters such as when you discuss (negotiate) with your spouse whether to cook and eat in or go out and eat in a restaurant. This might involve small exchange (negotiation) between a husband and wife, and it might go like this:

Wife (to her husband): what do you think dear if we eat out tonight?

Husband: Well, I do not like to eat out tonight; we just did that four days ago.

Wife: Yes, but the reason I want to eat out is because I am tired.

Husband: I will just heat up something in the house.

Wife: You know what I will cook something quick. Don't worry I will take care of it.

As you can see in this small negotiation scenario, the negotiation involved: 1- a subject matter: eating in the house or out- in a restaurant. 2- A communication media:

direct language. 3- A settlement: Wife agreed to cook, the negation case was closed successfully (Win – Win) and negotiation case was closed.

Another example of a negation on a large scale matter might involve two countries such as USA and China engaged in USA imposing 10% taxes on all Chinese imports into the USA (the subject matter).

This negotiation involves different people and governmental departments. However, the element (components) of the negotiation remains the same.

The negotiation might take a similar script as follows:

USA: we are going to impose 10% taxes on your export to USA.

China: It is not fair if you do that.

USA: We have no choice under the circumstances but impose this tax, we are sorry.

China: Then, we also will impose similarly taxes on your imports to China. You, also, left us no choice to impose tax.

Now, here is a negotiation case where the three elements are also clear (subject matter of negotiation, media of communication- in this case it could involve direct and indirect means such as letters, telephone, etc, and a settlement- no settlement yet).

Negotiation is an art, not an exact science such as mathematics, physics, or chemistry. Therefore, negotiation, as an art practiced by humans, requires that we become familiar with the areas of negotiation which I will call the major components of any negotiation. These components are:

1- Communication media

2- Subject matter at hand of the negotiation

3- Settlement.

Negotiation Skills

There are techniques and strategies when negotiating; here are some of the important ones:

1- Do Your Homework:

Know who you're negotiating with before you begin. What's his or her reputation as a negotiator? Win/Win model or Win/Lose model? Does the person want to negotiate with you, dread the negotiation, or is this a neutral situation.

2- Practice Double (put yourself in the other party's shoes)

It's not enough to know what you want out of negotiation. You also need to anticipate what the other party wants.

3- Build Trust

Negotiation is a highly sophisticated form of communication. Without trust, there won't be communication. Instead you'll have manipulation and suspicion masquerading as communication. Be trustworthy. Honor your commitments. Tell the truth. Respect confidences.

4-Develop External Listening

Most people carry on an inner dialogue with themselves. When you're trying to communicate with someone else, this inner dialogue becomes a problem because you can't listen internally and externally at the same time. When you negotiate, turn off your inner voice and only listen externally. You won't miss important nonverbal messages, facial expressions of voice inflections, when you listen externally.

5- Own Your Power

Don't assume that because the other party has one type of power, that he or she is all-powerful. That's giving away your power. Balance power by assessing the other parties source(s) of power, and then your own. While there are many sources of power, they all break down into two categories; internal power and external power. The former no one can take away from you and includes your personal power, level of self-esteem, and self-confidence. External power fluctuates with your situation. TIP is an acronym that stands for Time, Information, and Power. If you're laid off or demoted you can lose position power, for example. If new technology is introduced, you can lose your expertise power. Because the dynamics of power are so changeable, a negotiation is never dead. Be patient; the power dynamics may shift.

6- Know Your BATNA

BATNA stands for Best Alternative to A Negotiated Agreement. The acronym comes out of the research on negotiation conducted by the Harvard Negotiation Project. Before you begin a negotiation, know what your options are. Can you walk away from the deal? What other choices do you have? What are the pros and cons of each choice? Don't stop here. Also consider the BATNA of the other party.

7- Know What a Win Is

What is your best case scenario? What is your worst case scenario? The area in between is called your *settlement range*. If you can reach an agreement within your settlement range, that's a Win! Don't drop below your bottom line; you'll feel bad about yourself and the deal afterwards, and you may not follow-through on your commitments.

8-Enjoy the Process

Negotiation is a process, not an event. There are predictable steps: preparation, creating the climate, identifying interests, and selecting outcomesthat you will go through in any negotiation. With practice, you will gain skill at facilitating each step of the process. As your skill increases, you'll discover that negotiating can be fun. So, have fun and enjoy any negotiations.

Get rid of guilt now, and live happy forever

Guilt is a destructive emotion, and harmful feeling, if not treated and dealt with in a timely fashion.

Guilt comes (in other words we acquire the feeling of guilt) in two ways:

1. Externally- imposed guilt: this is when others accuse us of something we did do or something we did not do.

2. Internally- imposed guilt: This is the guilt we impose on ourselves. This is the worst type of guilt, because we, ourselves, believe that we are guilty of whatever we accuse ourselves of, and it is very hard to free ourselves from this kind of guilt.

Guilt is a temporary state of mind. Guilt is a destructive feeling when we do not resolve it in time, swiftly and properly.

Internal guilt is usually caused by our own belief that WE SHOULD HAVE ACTED OR DONE OR SHOULD NOT HAVE ACTED OR DONE or even THOUGHT of something.

We feel guilty because of our false belief that we had total control over all the situations we regretted, and now we feel that it was within our own total control and nobody else's. This premise and belief is wrong because we do not have total and complete control over all regrettable (guilt causing) incidents and events. Therefore, we should not feel guilty and bad, because most of the time we were not responsible for what happened or did not happen. Even when we commit real sins and we feel that we were responsible, there is always a way to redeem ourselves, and let go of the feeling of guilt. We can free ourselves of guilt by believing and convincing ourselves that feeling guilty will only hurt us and will not help anyone at all.

We only hurt ourselves when we think that we can redeem ourselves and pay our wrong doings by suffering or by believing that there is no way to forgive and redeem ourselves.

The challenge is not to surrender to inaction and passivity, but to courageously find a way to redeem and liberate ourselves and live free of guilt. Feeling guilty does not benefit us, feeling free does make us feel good and productive for ourselves and others as well. Let guilt go and get rid of it forever and be free; you deserve to live happy- it is your right to be happy and free of guilt. Pursuit of happiness, which means getting rid of any feelings that interfere with our happiness including the feeling of guilt, is your right. So, pursue your right to be happy and not feel guilty.

You can Succeed in your Life if you Think you can

How to Succeed in school, Work, marriage, society, and in all endeavors

A thought is the seed of any success ever known to mankind. For example, all the inventions and discoveries accomplished by man- from the invention of the wheel to modern computers- started with an idea in somebody's mind. Think and ask yourself right now where am I going? In others words, ask yourself: where am I going and how am I doing in my school? Where am I going in my current relationship? Where and how am I doing in my current job? In my business? In life in general? If you do not know where you are going you will be like a ship in the middle of the ocean with no direction. It will end up anywhere, probably on the rocks destroyed because of its lack of direction. You must set your goals and have a plan for your life to succeed, and succeed you will when you do what it takes to succeed:

In summary:

1) Think about what you want.

2) Set goals.

3) Plan action steps to accomplish what your goals are.

4) Take action to complete the steps you outlined. Without action nothing happens. You must harness all your mind potentials. It has been stated that all people use less than 4% of their brain power/potential, and you must use what knowledge you already possess. Use what knowledge you have and if indeed you need some more then by all means acquire it quickly and get on with activating your plan. Just do not fall into the trap of "I need more information to act"; this will make you a non-active/non-practical person because you always think that you need some more information to act. So just do it now. Having a well thought out and defined plan and its action steps lead us to the only conclusion and that is success. Having a definite purpose will help you concentrate; develop self-reliance and confidence, enthusiasm, initiative, imagination, and all the components necessary for success.

When you think and draw a specific plan and its action steps you basically separate an area in your life for action and specialization. Time must be allotted to achieving their actions on a day-to-day basis.

You will also be able to identify opportunities pertaining to your success because you know what you are looking for specifically and not in generalities.

Use the KFC formula to succeed and accomplish your purpose and goals.

KFC stands for KNOW what you want, FIND out what you are getting, and CHANGE what you are doing until you get what you want.

Decision-making is another skill that becomes natural once you have your plan and its action steps defined. The secret, however, to decision making lies in having courage in taking risks and not being afraid. Fear is the opposite of success. Therefore, make any decision with the facts you have right now and correct your decision later if needed because waiting for all the facts to come in will be a wait forever.

Have faith and believe in what you are doing. Belief in what you are doing will give you a positive attitude towards your goals and free you from the limitations of doubt, discouragement, indecision, and procrastination. Whatever you believe you will achieve.

Fear of failure can cause and lead to failure (self- fulfilling prophecy)

Even if we admit that a desire for self-esteem occasionally brings forth adverse effects, doesn't the average individual still derive much more benefit than harm through pursuing a positive self-image? Isn't the small price worth paying?

The answer to this question is, no, the price usually is *not* worth paying. The expense we incur for esteeming ourselves is by no means limited to feelings of humiliation when failing. If that were the case -- if the only unpleasant consequence of self-esteem were an occasional feeling of disgrace when failing -- then one could legitimately argue that self-esteem often benefits individuals who are exceptionally successful, attractive, or talented. If a person paints a breathtaking masterpiece or writes a bestselling novel, then surely he will esteem himself; and it is this sought-for feeling of glorification and achievement that seems to inspire many creative pursuits.

To a limited extent, the drive for self-esteem probably does drive some individuals to productive and creative activity. This reality, in fact, seems to be a popular "selling point" for self-esteem. Instead of stimulating genius and creativity, however, the theology and theory of self-esteem more often result in severe behavioral inhibition and debilitating anxiety. With his entire self-worth at stake, the average individual will desperately avoid all "dangerous" situations wherein his self-esteem is vulnerable to loss.

Take, for example, the average-looking, average-intelligence single male, who feels romantically and sexually attracted to a woman of extraordinary beauty and brilliance. This gentleman may daydream vividly about dating or marrying such a desirable woman and his self-esteem would no doubt be temporarily elevated if his fantasies were realized. But this man's self-rating philosophy -- i.e., his belief that self-worth flows from success -- virtually guarantees that he will never befriend the woman he considers most desirable. Why? Because his precious self-esteem would be destroyed if he were rejected openly by such an attractive, enticing female. He cannot "risk" the "danger." He will play it safe, asking out a less attractive, less intelligent woman. That way, the likelihood of rejection will decline, and the threat to his self-esteem will diminish.

This single male's *ego*, therefore, inhibited, rather than supported, his search for cultured female companionship. If he simply forgot the "danger" to his pride -- which of course is completely in his head and represents no actual danger in the empirical world -- then he could telephone the woman he truly desires and may indeed make her acquaintance. If she, nonetheless, rejects and rebuffs his advances, then he will naturally feel disappointed, but, because his entire value as a human being is not in jeopardy, he will *not* feel ashamed or humiliated.

When a person views himself as "worthless" and feels humiliated, he is then inclined to view himself as *incapable* of correcting his poor performances. He tends to give up, and to rationalize excuses for withdrawing from outside activities and interpersonal relationships. After all, he reasons, how could a worthless bum such as himself succeed at anything truly significant? On the other hand, if an individual views his current *behavior*, rather than himself, as deficient, then he clearly sees that, through more practice and effort, he may in the future rectify his previously deficient behavior. In other words, one must not take things personal.

Pause to ask yourself this question: Does your long nose or your poor complexion *really* prevent you from asking out highly desirable members of the opposite sex? Or is it, rather, your fear of ego-deflation that deters you from asking? Women, especially, should give careful thought to similar questions because, in our silly society, it is considered much more "risky" for a woman to ask out a man than vice versa.

Likewise, our self-esteem inhibits us from participating in any activity in which failure is deemed disgraceful. And because failure in virtually *any* endeavor is deemed disgraceful by the self-esteeming individual, he becomes distinctly afraid to try anything unfamiliar. He passively goes through life doing what he's always done -- rarely involving himself in enterprises and human relationships whose success is not guaranteed in advance. Far from inspiring productive behavior and social interaction, the concept of self-esteem is *the* most inhibiting philosophy imaginable. That "most men lead lives of quiet desperation" can perhaps be traced to our chilling fear of losing self-esteem and to our resulting tendency toward a mundane, routine existence.

Self-esteem usually promotes social and behavioral inhibition, because of the fear of failure of losing your pride (self-esteem). It is a self-fulfilling prophesy and you get what you expect- if you expect failure you usually get failure and if you expect success you will get success.

Deal with Fear courageously, and regain your joy of living

The fear of death is the most unjustified of all fears, for there's no risk of accident for someone who's dead.

Albert Einstein

The only thing we have to fear is fear itself.

Franklin D. Roosevelt

Control fear or it will control you

Fear is number one enemy to us; we are born with an innate and intrinsic fear. When we were babies we got scared whenever we heard a loud sound, or when we did not get our food. Fear was always part of our lives. Our parents, sometimes, tried to alleviate our fears by feeding us, cuddling and hugging, or by simply smiling and pampering us gently, and in response we felt secure (unafraid) and safe, at least temporarily and at that moment.

However, as we grew up and started interacting with other children and adults, we started acquiring the "learned" fears, even with our own families (parents, sisters, brothers, and relatives) began punishing us for any mistakes we made.

We were taught, at least in most cultures, to fear God, our parents, the elderly, and the authorities (police, teachers, etc). Therefore, we developed a "learned" and very dangerous fear of people and we became slaves to this abysmal and deep feeling of fear.

Therefore, we must admit and accept that we were programmed to be scared constantly, but we must overcome and transcend all or at least most of these fears. We must see the fears as a normal part of our lives. However, we must control our reactions and not let fear control us and cause ulcers, headaches, and all kind of physical problems.

We must see fear as part of life, and in fact fear can be a motivator when it does not become excessive. There is an oxymoronic adage that says "fear is safety".

Control your reaction to your fears by not saying things under anger and fear. And by not acting under fear by hitting or doing regrettable things, and you will control your life. Happiness relies on your ability to control your fear.

Have no fear of anything or anybody

Nothing is scarier than leaving your mother's stomach when you were born to face the world of the unknown and uncertainty, but you survived that fear. Every parent remembers when they held their first newly born child (I certainly do remember vividly holding my first child) in their arms. You felt scared and helpless. You just kept crying and perhaps praying not to be hurt, you held on to dear life's thin strings.

This is a lesson for you and all of us. Life is not to be feared, but faced head on without preconceived fear, sometimes others love to implant in us.

Have no fear and be courageous, you will win and will be happy. Just thrust ahead and never look back or go backward, that is defeat. Winners are not afraid to face their fears and conquer them, you are a winner once you do that and believe it. Sometimes things will go against you, and things seem to go completely wrong and all odds are against you. Keep your faith strong no matter what happened. Think of these times as a test of your strength and your well.

Some people are not fair in dealing with you, that's ok, because life is not perfect, nor is it fair sometimes. But, remember that everything in time shall pass, good or bad. Just hang in there strong and do not give up.

When you give up that is when you lose. you are not, and do want to, and will not be a loser and failure, because you are not a failure until you stop trying.

You did not come this far to be a looser because of a vicious attack or anything in this life.

Make Friends with Fear; it can work for you

It makes sense to ASSUME that those bold enough to take big chances must be unusually self-confident and have no FEAR. But it isn't so. Many of the towering figures we look up to are no less afraid than anyone else. They just don't let fear immobilize or distract them.

Plenty of prominent people have carried on despite near-crippling anxieties. Legendary football coach Bear Bryant often gave up the contents of his stomach before big games. So did Sir Laurence Olivier before his many stage performances. Winston Churchill, one of history's greatest orators, suffered such stage fright that he'd rehearse his speeches obsessively.

Even former President Ronald Reagan never conquered his speech-making nerves. According to Reagan speechwriter Peggy Noonan, the real reason he told so many jokes at the outset of speeches wasn't so much to humor the audience, but to ease his own anxiety.

We're too quick to assume that fear leads to failure, says Richard Farson, who has studied the topic at length. Actually, when fear doesn't paralyze it can be a motivator. High achievers see fear as a necessary evil at worst, and at best a valuable ally.

"Those who are paralyzed by the thought of taking a chance see only peril in fear's crackling flames," he said in "Whoever Makes the Most Mistakes Wins."

"They imagine themselves being burned at the stake and back off. Those who see energy in terror's heat convert fear into fuel. To them, it looks like an exciting bonfire."

It isn't fear's intensity that determines our ability to act. Rather, it's the approach we take towards feeling afraid. When faced with danger, everyone recoils. That's natural. But don't fall into the trap of waiting for fear to subside before acting.

The late boxing manager Cus D'Amato used to tell his fighters that fear was their best friend, Farson says. Boxers who weren't scared enough let their minds wander. An ability to pay full attention to the task at hand is enhanced by fear.

Improved focus is fear's most valuable byproduct. It can work to the benefit of the boxer in physical jeopardy, the business leader taking on financial risk and the public speaker facing social scrutiny.

Performers of all kinds, energized by their fear of confronting an audience, convert their fear to energy and focus. Luciano Pavarotti said it was concentration, more than voice, that made a singer great. "I like 'nervous' in a performance," he once said.

At the same time, fear shouldn't be seen as something that needs to be conquered or even ignored, Farson says. It's too valuable a commodity. "We get scared for a reason. It tells us when to be alert. Fear is a gift to our spirits for the same reason pain is essential to our health."

Arctic explorer Peter Freuchen agreed with that line of thinking. "I do what I can to get away from those fellows who never get scared. They are very dangerous men. They get you into all kinds of trouble – those fellows who are scared of nothing. They die soon. I am always scared."

There is also another adage that states: anyone who does not fear others, or God, or the law is dangerous, and must be FEARED and watched.

Feelings and emotions are not facts

Feeling that something is a fact does not make it so, most of the time. The truth is that feelings do not change facts. Therefore, feelings most of the time are not true (facts). Feeling depressed does not really make you depressed

For example, feeling dumb does not change the fact you have a good mind. Feeling ugly does not change the fact you have a reasonably attractive body. Feelings like you are the greatest does not change the fact there are others who can do certain things better than you can. Feeling depressed and down does not imply that you are indeed down and depressed.

All of these feelings are ephemeral and short-lived states of mind. They do not last. They are simply temporary conditions we hold in our minds until we acquire new feelings and replace the old states of our minds with the new ones. For example, suppose you feel sad and depressed because you do not have any money, and out of desperation, you decide to play the lottery, and you win a million dollars. How do you feel now? Probably, you feel very happy. You can see how your feelings of depression and sadness instantly disappeared, and were replaced by feeling of joy and happiness.

Keep your emotions in balance by keeping in mind that all feelings (anger, depression, jealousy, etc) are only thoughts stored in your mind for the time being and temporary until other feelings replace them. By balancing your emotional life, you will regain your joy in life.

You can control your behavior, but you CAN NOT control your Emotions

Your emotions provide you with useful information to help you better control your thoughts and your actions. Emotion itself, however, is not to be controlled. Trying to control, alter, or ignore your feelings is like putting tape over your car's instruments so you would not have to be bothered by them. By doing so you would miss out on valuable, even critical information, necessary to drive safely. Another example of trying to stop and control emotions is like trying to stop a hurricane from moving. We cannot control our emotions, and we should not even try. However, we must control our reactions (our behavior) to our emotions. By paying attention to your feelings--your emotional instruments--rather than trying to control them, you are in a better position to more effectively control yourself. With better self-control you generally feel better.

In a nut shell, you must <u>acknowledge and honor</u> all your emotions as valid and legitimate, and <u>accept</u> them as part of your existence, just like you accepted your feelings and urges of HUNGER, SLEEP, and TIREDENESS. Remember how you behaved under those circumstances. It is obvious that the right response is not to deny our hunger, but to satisfy it appropriately.

By the same analogy, you must not ignore your feelings of anger, jealousy, frustration, etc, but you must behave and respond to these feeling in a suitable manner, and not submitting to them by acting irrationally.

The following insights will help you set a solid foundation for managing your emotions and moving ahead your life.

1. Learn and discover rather than defend. Instead of going into a defensive mode and trying to protect or force your views, learn from the state of affairs at hand. The old saying is true, "When you change someone's point-of-view against their will, you've never truly changed them." From the moment you lose control and retaliate (even if you are right) you've lost the battle. However, by controlling your emotions and investigating the other's viewpoint, you open yourself to a calm and enlightening discussion.

2. Acknowledge rather than be in agreement. It is possible to acknowledge that someone has a different point-of-view than you have without agreeing with their point-of-view. What happens, is that the more strongly someone disagrees with us, the more adamant we become about convincing them we are right. Before the situation gets out of control, ask yourself, "How important is it that they agree with me?" If

the answer comes down to a matter of personal pride - let it go. Acknowledge and respect other's views, the fact that you have a conflicting opinion and allow the conversation to drift to another topic.

3. Express your emotions. Expressing empathy and being emotionally honest is one of the things that will make you a true leader. Everyone you work with already knows you are human. When you share your strengths, weaknesses, triumphs and trials honestly with those around you, you make a more personal connection.

4. Stay in integrity with your values. Emotional control does not equate to silence. Just the opposite. When a difficult subject needs to be addressed, you will be fully able to do so with a level head. When the truth needs to be told, you will be a person other's look to. By showing others you are filled with integrity and you stand by your values will help to define your reputation. Respect always follow those whose "yes" means "yes" and whose "no" means "no".

5. Diplomatically handle the negative. It seems, regardless the size of organization you work for, that negative people will always be present. These are the ones that continually complain, create confrontations and lack control of their emotions.

DIFFERENCES BETWEEN EMOTIONAL BEHAVIOR (ACTION) AND EMOTIONS (FEELING)

It is easy to confuse emotional behavior, which is best controlled within some reasonable bounds, with emotion, itself. Although behavior such as fighting or fleeing may express emotion, it is not emotion itself. Emotion, for the most part, is simply the body's *internal* reaction to what is going on in the mind. It occurs internally as opposed to behavior which is external.

There is a distinct difference between the appropriate control of emotional behavior (controlling what you say or do when you feel angry) and the counterproductive attempt to control emotion (ignoring or fighting the feeling of anger). Although struggling to control the stream of emotion may seem natural, it is healthier to focus on and control the thoughts and actions that direct the flow of the stream, rather than focusing on the stream itself (emotions).

Control Your Behavior and Become a Happy and Successful Leader

If you want to succeed in life you must know your true self. The ability to listen to our own emotions, wants, desires and needs is as important as listening to others. This is the first step for everything and for anybody who wants to make a difference in his or her life. In addition, putting the understanding of your emotions (and those of others) into practice is equally important.

There are times all of us want to lash out at our superiors or peers for violating our boundaries, interfering with our affairs, crossing the line, stepping behind our backs, talking behind us, or taking advantage of us in some way.

Those are only natural feelings. Everyone has had them from time to time. However, what you DO (your reactions/actions) with those feelings and emotions is what counts. Controlling your anger and frustration and learning to perform more productively and in a smart way under stressful circumstances is the defining factor.

Unfortunately, changing your emotional response to others is considered a "lifestyle change". And, as we all know, those are the most difficult to implement and maintain. If changing unproductive habits were as simple as being aware of them, we'd all be living ideal lives. Changing habits and behaviors takes more than awareness and self-knowledge. This is why traditional training (such as books, audio tapes, video training and workshops) often falls short in creating long-term change. They don't offer a consistent support system... the one thing that is vital to maintaining new behaviors (making it a habit).

I recommend that you find a mentor or coach to assist with this process. After all, there is an elegant beauty apparent in people that can remain calm when no one else can. Aristotle said, "Anyone can become angry - that is easy. But to be angry with the right person, to the right degree, at the right time, for the right purpose, in the right way - this is not easy."

The insights below will help you lay down a solid foundation for managing your emotions, or rather your reaction to them) and progressing forward in your career.

1. Learn rather than defend. Instead of going into a defensive mode and trying to protect or force your views, learn from the situation. Ask yourself what is really going on with that upset employee or coworker. The old saying is true, "When you change someone's point-of-view against their will, you've never truly changed them." Or the other famous saying "A person

changed against his will is of the same opinion still". From the moment you lose control and retaliate (even if you are right) you've lost the battle. However, by controlling your reactions to your emotions and investigating the other's viewpoint, you open yourself to a calm and enlightening discussion.

2. Acknowledge rather than agree. It is possible to acknowledge that someone has a different point-of-view than you have without agreeing with their point-of-view. What happens, more often than not, is that the more strongly someone disagrees with us, the more adamant we become about convincing them we are right. Before the situation gets out of control, ask yourself, "How important is it that they agree with me?" If the answer comes down to a matter of personal pride - let it go. Acknowledge and respect other's views, the fact that you have a conflicting opinion and allow the conversation to drift to another topic.

3. Express your emotions. Expressing empathy and being emotionally honest is one of the things that will make you a true leader. Everyone you work with already knows you are human. When you share your strengths, weaknesses, triumphs and trials honestly with those around you, you make a more personal

connection. Let us never forget, people follow those they like. While your primary concern at the office may not be to make friends; opening yourself up to your team will help develop a sense of trust and loyalty towards you.

4. Stay in integrity with your values- Practice and do what you say. Emotional control does not equate to silence. When a difficult subject needs to be addressed, you will be fully able to do so... with a level and calm head. When the truth needs to be told, you will be a person others look to. By showing others you are filled with integrity and you stand by your values will help to define your reputation. Respect always follow those whose "yes" means "yes" and whose "no" means "no", as I stated earlier.

5. Tactfully handle the negative. It seems, regardless of the size of the organization you work for, that negative people will always be present. These are the ones that continually complain, create confrontations and lack control of their emotions. If their contribution to your team does not outweigh the damaging attitude, you may want to consider having them transferred to a position where they would be more suited. Be aware of these personality types. Also be prepared to

handle the challenges they will bring to you as you prepare to develop your new emotional steadiness.

Learning how to control yourself (your reactions to your emotions) will enable you to be a good and progressive leader. Progressive leaders are emotionally stable leaders. They are the ones others turn to during a crisis. They are the ones that become the beacon and guide of true leadership. They are the ones that make it to the top!

Get to know your emotions and how to manage them under pressure, and you will be a happy leader others look up to and respect.

Control your reactions to your emotions by breathing properly

The connection between emotions and breathing generally goes unnoticed, though we see and observe it in ourselves and in others every day. When we are emotional, breathing is on the "automatic pilot." As we are focused on the object of our emotion, we hardly ever consciously register the close relationship between emotions and breathing. When we are angry, fearful, or anxious, we over-breathe or as one would say in common jargon, we "gasp and blow", or huff and puff.

In case of sadness, suspense, conflict or depression, we under-breathe, "hold our breath," so to speak. These changes in the breathing are automatic. Incidentally, there is a chain reaction of other physical changes that take place automatically, such as the release of chemicals, sympathetic, and parasympathetic nervous system activity which accompany the changes in the breathing rate. Why do I choose to talk about the relationship between emotions and breathing? Because breathing is a unique bodily function which can be "automatic," that is, it can function on its own, without our deliberate effort to breathe and it can also be a conscious, "self directed," and voluntary activity.; controllable to a degree.

When we bring breathing under our direct and voluntary control, we can use it as a tool to control emotions. We can easily observe the changes in our breathing when we consciously attempt to do so. It is difficult, if not impossible to observe and control the chemical and neurophysiological changes that take place inside our body, but, with just a little training and steady awareness, we can easily influence and change our breathing.

Similarly, it is extremely difficult to directly influence the activity of our heart, kidney, stomach, intestines, and other organs which are involved in the experiencing of emotions. Through breathing, we can influence the activity of these internal organs. While the negative emotions cause over-breathing, under-breathing, and other irregular breathing activity, the positive emotions cause breathing to be deeper, easier, and effortless. By the same functional relationship, when we restore our breathing to a deep, smooth, and rhythmical pattern, we can reduce the strength of negative emotions and acquire a peaceful and relaxing mental state.

Nature has equipped us with a "fight or flight" emergency response for survival against the enemy or danger. It has also provided us with a "calming" response, to restore peace and serenity, equally important for our survival. You can trigger a calming response whenever you like by pressing the 'button, labeled breathing" i.e. your breathing. *Take five or ten deep, smooth, rhythmical breathes. With each breathe out, say the word "calm" or "relax," or "love" silently in your head and there you are!* You have triggered *a calming response*. It is simple and effective, most of the times.

Other times, if there is a lot of muscular tension or 'heat" generated by the emotions, you may not be physically and mentally ready to go into a calm state unless you *move* your body a little bit. *That is what the word, "E-motion" conveys. Emotion puts you in a state of motion, stirred up, excited or agitated.* So, if you find yourself in such a state, it might be good to first move your body a little bit. Do just a few push- ups, jumping in place, or jog lightly to dissipate the tension and to extend the "energy" accumulated. It would then be more beneficial to do the deep, rhythmical, smooth breathing. Norman Vincent Peale tells a story of a man, who in the midst of an argument with his colleagues, walks up to a couch and lies down. His arguing colleagues, curious of this strange behavior, ask him what he is doing and whether he is suddenly taken ill. The man tells them that he went to lie down because he was getting angry and it is difficult for him to get angry if he is lying down. There is a great lesson in this story for all of us. Take a preventative action! Don't let ourselves get too stirred up by the emotion. When an emotion begins to get hold of you, take a mental note on how you are breathing and right away go back to belly breathing. You will be in control of the situation and think clearly. It can prevent you from saying or doing things that you might regret later.

Breathe properly or Get Sick and lose control

Proper breathing is an important component of a healthy physical and mental life. In fact, breathing is equated with life. The word "Spirit" is derived from "spirare" which means to breathe.

Many fundamental actions are derived from the action of breathing. A person is "inspired" by ideas, "aspires" to a higher goal, and "expires" when the last breath is out. Such was the importance given to breathing by our ancestors. We breathe about twelve to eighteen breaths in a minute which comes to about 18,000 to 26,000 breaths every twenty-four hours.

Nature starts us off with the correct way of breathing, which is the diaphragmatic breathing. Look at babies during the first year of their life when they are lying on their backs. As babies breathe in, their tummy rises like they are inflating a beach ball inside their tummies. When they breathe out, the "beach ball" caves in. This occurs because of the use of the diaphragm in breathing.

The diaphragm is a dome shaped muscle in the midsection, over the stomach and intestines and under the heart and lungs. It is like a dividing layer between the lower and upper sections of our torso. When you breathe in, the dome shaped diaphragm caves in to allow the lungs to be filled by air. When you breathe out, the "dome" moves up to push air out of the lungs.

How much oxygen you take in with your breath and how much carbon dioxide you give off when you breathe out depends on how actively your diaphragm is involved in the breathing process. To appreciate the full impact of this statement, reconsider the information that we breathe, on average, about eighteen to twenty-six thousand times a day. So, even if you take just a little more oxygen each time you breathe in, it adds up in a day's time. This will have a beneficial effect on physical and mental health.

You can do this little observation on yourself to check your own pattern of breathing:

Sit in a quiet place and just settle down for a minute or two. Put your hand, horizontally, about one inch above your navel. Close your eyes. Breathe normally without trying to influence your breathing one way or the other. Observe how your tummy moves every time you breathe in and breathe out. If you are breathing correctly, you should find that the hand over the tummy moves as you breathe in and out.

As stated earlier, abdominal breathing is a correct way of breathing. If your chest is moving as you breathe in and out, and you do not have a medical reason to do so, that means that you are breathing shallowly and incorrectly. Having checked yourself for the abdominal breathing, now you may check if your tummy is moving in the right pattern.

Close your eyes again. The tummy should move out when you breathe inn and go in when you breathe out. If that is not happening, and for example, your tummy moves in when you breathe in, you can easily correct it.

Take a slow, deep breath in and breathe out slowly and steadily. The next breath will come in automatically, that is without your effort. Your tummy will move outward as you breathe in and move inward as you breathe out. If you lose it again, no problem. Take a deep, slow, easy breath and blow it out, slowly and steadily. Do it as many times as you need to. It will only make it better for you.

As you begin to pay steady attention to your breathing, it will be easier for you to monitor your breathing. Any time you find yourself holding your breath or having a jerky breath, breathing irregular or faster, just go back to your belly breathing. So, start right now breathing properly; give your body the oxygen it needs, and exhale (expire) the carbon monoxide from your system, and ultimately You can Regain control of Your Life and Be Happy Again healthily.

Chapter # 6 — Things that you cannot control; just accept them

Wisdom of what you can change

Wisdom is the ability of DISTINGUISHING and Learning the difference between what you are thinking and what the real reality is. When something negative comes to mind, realize first that it's only a thought. Then, ask yourself, is this something I have power over? If what came up is beyond your control, be ready to reply, this is something I can't change, I am going to JUST LET GO, since I cannot control it.

It all begins with your ability to differentiate between your thinking and what's really going on in the world around you. To know that a thought is just a thought is at first troubling, then extraordinarily and very liberating.

When you desire something, you start working hard toward attaining and getting whatever it is you want.

Similarly, you try to stay away from those things you have an aversion to. If you don't get what you hope for, it's unfortunate, but if you get what you're trying to steer clear of and DO NOT WANT, you experience misfortune. That's why you should confine your avoidance to things within your control, so you'll never experience misery. Because, if you try to avoid sickness, death, solving daily problems such as arguing with a spouse and anybody else whom you must interact with or poverty, then sooner or later you're sure to run into them, and BECOME VERY FRUSTRATED, UNHAPPY, and the JOY OF LIVING starts to fade away.

Do not waste your energy on what you have no power (control) over; instead, use your energy in areas where you have authority and power. However, don't try to escape circumstances and events that you can change, by some means. Life becomes very easy then, and hope instead of frustration becomes your philosophy and your future will be bright as the shining moon, and ultimately the sun rise will bring you JOY OF LIVING.

Nothing lasts forever, everything shall pass

Everything shall pass; just think how each day comes and goes by and becomes passé, how a month comes, and then a whole year comes and they all pass, and again they all become the past. One day, one month, and one year all come and pass as if they never were here. Nothing lasts forever, whether it is good or bad; they all pass. There is solace, relief, and comfort in this fact of "nothing lasts forever, and everything shall pass".

Everyone goes through hard and bad times, but you know they shall pass. As long as you realize that indeed everything passes and become a memory, then you will hang in there and stay strong, because you know that all things will pass, since nothing lasts forever.

It is hard sometimes to really see the light at the end of tunnel and keep hope alive, when things get tough and we are not used to handling and managing hard times. Our hopes, dreams, and even our entire future starts to become questionable, bleak, and not as we want to see it or expect it to be. We start doubting and second guessing ourselves, and the people we love and who love us. We create confusion, doubt, turmoil, and disharmony in our lives.

The right response, in these tough and hard times, is to stand strong and accept the fact that these hard times shall pass and today will become yesterday, and good thing are ahead of us, because there is always hope for better things to come. Furthermore, all these hard times make us stronger and more adaptable to the twists (changes of life). Just keep in mind that nothing lasts forever; everything shall pass, and good things are ahead of us to come as well as joy of living.

Chapter # 7 — Face Problems and Solve them and don't avoid them

Problems/ challenges and how to deal with them intelligently

"We can't solve problems by using the same kind of thinking we used when we created them."

Albert Einstein

Do not ignore your PROBLEMS, Acknowledge their existence

What Is a Problem?

Let us define what a problem is. A problem is defined (when using critical thinking) as an issue/question or circumstance/situation that calls for a solution.

It simply means that when you encounter a problem, you can take action or make effectual decisions that will result in the resolution of that problem- after you define the REAL and TRUE problem, of course.

Different problems require different solutions. The type of the problem at hand dictates the desired solution.

Question Problems: based on this problem definition, problems that happen in the form of a question are usually those that do not have one simple answer. Such as: Why do you like French food more than American food?

Situational problems:

Situational problems require critical thinking and making decisions about the best way of action. For example, you discover that your spouse is cheating on you. Actions you might consider would include: 1- simply file for divorce after you have all the evidence you need that cheating took place OR 2- Instead of filing for divorce, you confront and discuss the situation with your spouse and find out why the cheating took place, and negotiate and take it from there.

Barriers to Recognizing a Problem

The most universal reason for not recognizing a problem is the desire to evade taking action or responsibility. The rational and thinking behind ignoring the problem is based on the assumption that no acknowledgment (no acceptance of the existence of the problem) means no accountability for solving THE PROBLEM at hand. For example, when you fail a test, you blame other factors other than yourself such as the teacher, the text book, the weather, or anything else. You made this decision to avoid taking responsibility. Obviously, if you took responsibility you will be able to correct the test problem by taking constructive action such as studying harder and smarter.

Realize that by not admitting your problem, you make the solution extremely difficult and even impossible to resolve. The first problem could grow bigger and more complex, and by not taking action and just by waiting you could create multiple problems that need complex solutions. In summary, the failure to recognize a problem almost always creates more complex work for you.

Types of problems

After you acknowledge that a problem exists, you should determine the type of problem as it relates to a timeframe and your personal priorities. There are two criteria to use in your determination: severity and significance of the problem:

Severe Problems

These problems may be identified by the following:

1- Require immediate solutions and attention.

2- May require the involvement of others who have more expertise than you.

3- May result in even more drastic consequence if not resolved timely.

For example, when your blood pressure goes 50 % above normal, you know that this is a serious and severe problem that needs immediate attention and no delay in finding out why and solving it.

Delays can result in more complications and difficult problems and physical and mental issues to deal with and also costly solutions. You might even end up with a heart attack.

Some minor problems can become very severe if not solved immediately.

Defining the Real Problem (Real vs. Perceived Problem)

Whatever issue you face, the only way to come up with the right solution is to identify the real problem that needs to be solved before you can do anything else. If you don't, you could end up spending your time treating the consequence and symptoms of your problem while the real problem remains waiting to be resolved. You must learn how to differentiate between real problems and perceived problems (those most immediately apparent) and understand the most common reasons for missing true problems. Only when you define the issue you must resolve can you then begin to work on a solution.

Have you ever wasted time trying to find a solution to something, only to find out that the real problem was still there, waiting for you? Maybe you spent money and time trying to make friends with someone who was acting badly and in a hostile manner towards you. What you failed to notice was that the person had problems that have nothing to do with you, and what you did; trying to gain or regain their friendship is totally useless. You really do not know why your friend is acting until you ask him or her why?

This scenario represents a common mistake in problem solving. People mistake the more obvious symptoms or consequences of a problem for the actual problem. This happens for many reasons.

For example, you could be very busy, so whatever bothers you mostly; gets your attention without much thought about whether it is the real problem or not. Or, you may make assumptions about the nature of your problem and act on them rather than determining first if they are valid and true.

Two common results occur when you "solve" something that is not your actual problem.

1. Your solution will be wrong. (It fails to address the real problem.)

2. More complicated decisions will have to be made to solve the real problem later.

What Is the Actual (Real) Problem?

Most of the time the real problem facing you is hard to determine. For example, your boss gives you a bad evaluation (which results in no raise for you), and you wonder is it because he or she simply does not like you or because of your performance, or perhaps it is because of budget problems. In this case, defining the real problem requires some work to find out the real reason why your boss gave you a bad review.

You should ask yourself if your performance has been up to par because it could be simply due to your performance and nothing else, and if it is due to your poor performance, then the problem is poor performance and its solution is in your hands (improve your performance). If your performance has been good, then you need to ask him or her and find out the true problem.

At other times, your problem may seem devastating in its size and complexity. You may avoid dealing with it completely because you think you do not have energy or the time to deal with such a complex problem. However, when you take a closer look, there may be only one real problem, and a number of branches (offshoots) of that problem which will resolve themselves once you solve the actual problem.

How do you define the real problem?

You would need to do the following:

1- Get the information you need using any sources, including asking others, superiors, subordinates, and any resourceful people.

2- Do not be derailed into solving offshoots, or other consequences or symptoms of your problem instead of the problem itself.

3- Do not be overwhelmed and paralyzed when you are faced with a problem that looks like, or what you have been told is, a monstrous problem.

4- Think that you can solve the problem- because in fact you can, and you will be able to solve it.

Brainstorming to solve problems

Everyone has problems and challenges that need solving; they're an inevitable part of living. What many people don't realize, however, is that most of them can be overcome using a simple, focused program of personal brainstorming. Here are some practical tips to help you increase the effectiveness of your personal problem-solving skills:

Step 1: State your problem clearly

Before you start, firmly plant in your mind the idea that your problem can and will be solved. Your job is to find that solution, using personal or group brainstorming. State your problem clearly and concisely in one sentence at the top of a blank sheet of paper. Then, write down everything you know about your current problem or challenge. Try to isolate and write down specific factors or trends that have contributed to it. Keep in mind that a problem, clearly defined, is already half solved.

By gathering all of the information that you know about your challenge and placing it in front of you in tangible form, you enable your most powerful problem-solving tool- your brain- to see connections, interrelationships and implications in the information you've collected, which would not be obvious if you just kept all of this information in your head.

Think about people who have faced problems or challenges similar to the one you are facing. What strategies or solutions did they use? Then, determine if any elements of their solutions can be adapted to your current situation.

Step 2: Brainstorm solutions

As you review your problem statement and supporting information, write down any ideas that occur to you. Don't censor or criticize yourself at this point; there will be plenty of time to evaluate your ideas later. Write down every idea, no matter how far-fetched. Your goal at this stage of the personal brainstorming process is to generate a large quantity of ideas.

Ask yourself: How would a person who is an expert in this area solve this problem? You might want to try this exercise using famous people from history, creative thinkers such as Albert Einstein, or other leaders and innovators that you respect. Your goal for this exercise is to whack your thinking into a different frame of reference to generate fresh ideas and insights.

Divide your problem into its component pieces and write each of them down -- perhaps in a mind map or outline that shows the relationships between each element. Then, try brainstorming ideas for each one. This "slice and dice" technique often works well when you're faced with complex or multi-dimensional challenges.

Look ahead, and envision an ideal future goal or outcome. Then work backwards to the present, writing down the steps you would need to take now to move toward that objective.

If you find yourself running out of ideas too quickly, don't give up. Keep working at it until you have written down at least 20 possible ideas or solutions. Many times, the first 5 to 10 ideas you write down are top-of-mind solutions; often the best ideas take more concentrated and prolonged brainstorming to emerge.

Conclusion:

Your subconscious mind likes closure. When faced with an incomplete picture, it works to complete the mental image by inferring the missing information. Your mind works the same way on an unsolved problem or challenge; it loves to dive right in and get the job done.

In conclusion, remember that you can solve your problems and capitalize on new opportunities using your personal ideation and creativity. All you need is a pencil, a pad of paper and a quiet "thinking place" to tap into your creative muse and goddess of new ideas. Do it now. Get a pencil and start writing: define and write what the problem is first. And, follow all the above outlined steps until you find a suitable solution, and put a closure to the problem at hand.

Face problems, don't avoid them

When you have a problem, small or big, always try to solve it swiftly.

Compiling and accumulating problems only makes life seem harder.

Take life one day at a time and solve problems as they occur, it is not hard when you laugh at problems, and just have the courage to solve each one separately. Having courage to face reality and deal with the unpleasant things is the shortest and easiest way for you to be happy, and happiness is your right. Just do not postpone today's problem until tomorrow, because tomorrow will have its own challenges. Taking life one day at a time; solving one problem at a time will bring you JOY OF LIVING.

Chapter # 8 — Stress Can be Good, but it can be Devastating and harmfull

How to manage it to regain your joy of living

Stress: its sources, and how to manage it effectively

What are sources of stress?

1- Change of any kind can induce stress because of many reasons such as:

Fear of the new, the unknown

Feelings of personal insecurity

Feelings of vulnerability and helplessness

Fear of rejection

Need for approval

Lack of tolerance for ambiguity and uncertainty

2- Individual personality characteristics that can induce stress include:

Low self-esteem

Feelings of over-responsibility

Fear of loss of control

Fear of failure, error, mistakes

Fear of being judged

Lack of belief in ``being good enough"

Chronic striving to be "perfect'"

Chronic guilt

Unresolved grief over a loss or a series of losses

Chronic anger, hostility, or depression

3- Interpersonal issues that can induce stress

Interpersonal issues that can induce stress include:

Lack of adequate support within the relationship.

A lack of healthy communication within the relationship.

A sense of competitiveness between the parties involved

Threats of rejection or disapproval between people

An inability to be appropriately assertive

Struggle for power and control in the relationship

Poor intimacy or sexuality within the relationship

Chronic conflict and disagreement with no healthy resolution

Over dependency of one party on another

A troubled person who refuses to recognize the need for help

4- System issues that can induce stress

System (family, job, school, club, organization) issues that can induce stress include:

Lack of leadership

Lack of sense of direction

Uncooperative atmosphere

Competitive atmosphere

Autocratic leadership

Unclear expectations

A chronic sense of impending doom

A lack of teamwork

Confused communications

Developmental disability or chronic ill health of one or more members.

Is all stress bad?

Not all stress is distress and bad: a certain amount of stress or pressure is necessary and shows a positive adaptation being made by a person. This is called *eustress* (good stress).

Bad or negative stress is called *distress*: the negative physiological and emotional response when stress is intense and unresolved.

There are three degrees of stress:

Low: This is *distress* leading to boredom, fatigue, frustration, or dissatisfaction.

Optimum: This is *eustress* leading to creativity, problem solving, progress, change, learning, and energetic satisfaction.

High: Self- esteem, and irrational problem solving.

What is the definition of stress?

Stress is defined as a person's response to his environment. Stress is measured in terms of arousal or stimulation. As such, stress must be present for a person to function.

Each person has his own normal (homeostatic) level of arousal at which he functions best. If something unusual in the environment occurs, this level of arousal is affected.

There are three phases of arousal:

Phase 1. Alarm phase: When an unusual (or stressful) event occurs, the output of energy drops for a short period as the event is registered in the person's mind.

Phase 2. Adaptation phase: Next, the output of energy increases above the normal level; arousal is heightened as the person seeks to deal with the situation. Adaptation responses available to humans include physically running away, fighting, freezing (self immobilization), suppression emotion, or learning.

Phase 3. Exhaustion phase: Finally the person's available energy is expended and his capacity to function effectively is reduced.

The signs of physical response include:

Increased: heart rate, blood pressure, respiration, perspiration, pupil dilation, muscle tension. In the state of chronic stress, heart rate, blood pressure, and respiration are chronically elevated

The signs of physical response include:

Decreased: heart rate, blood pressure, respiration, pupil dilation, muscle tension

Stress management strategy is to evoke the relaxation physical response on a regular, daily basis.

Common stress related illnesses include:

Coronary artery disease

Peptic ulcer

Mental Illness

How high is your stress level?
Table of life events and their stress level

To learn the level of stress (distress) in your life, *circle* the value at the right of each of the following events if it has occurred within the past 12 months:

Event.. Value

Death of spouse..100

Divorce 73

Marital separation 65

Jail term 63

Death of close family member....................63

Personal injury or illness...........................53

Marriage...50

Fired from job 47

Marital reconciliation 45

Retirement 45

Change in family member's health.............44

Pregnancy...40

How to analyze your score:

Add the circled values. If your total score is more than 150, find ways to reduce stress in your daily life so that your stress level doesn't increase. The higher the score, the harder one needs to work at staying physically well.

Suggested uses for personal *Life Events* analysis:

Become familiar with the different events and the amounts of stress they promote.

Put the list of events where your family can easily refer to it several times a day.

What is personal progressive relaxation?

Learning to relax:

You may have grown to accept a certain high level of stress and anxiety as ``normal." You may be unfamiliar with what it feels like to be relaxed, calm, and unstressed.

With progressive relaxation you learn what it feels like to be relaxed, you learn to increase relaxation to a new level. By doing this you not only improve your physical well being by reducing hypertension, headaches, and other physical complaints, but you improve your mental state by reducing stress, anxiety, irritability, and depression.

The physical setting:

Progressive relaxation should take place in a quiet, attractive room. You should be completely supported. There should be no need for exertion to maintain body support. You should wear comfortable, loose fitting clothing during the sessions.

The process:

Lie on the floor or a bed and follow the directions of the relaxation technique in the following Relaxation Training Technique as you tense and relax various muscle groups. After the initial tensing of the muscles, release the tension instantly and completely. This is very important in order to get the ``pendulum effect.'' The muscles relax beyond the point of their normal relaxed state. You should then feel the important difference between tension and relaxation. You should concentrate on the feeling of relaxation; learn what it is to relax and how to increase it.

Continually repeat to yourself, ``Know what it feels like to be relaxed, deepen the relaxation, know what it is to be relaxed."

Do's and don'ts" of relaxation:

Do: Make sure you have comfortable, loose clothing and proper back support

Don't: Put yourself in an awkward position or in a position that will make it easy to fall asleep

Do: Allow your mind to quiet down. If tense thoughts enter while you are relaxing, let them pass out of your head.

Don't: Think your way into tension. If you can't clear your mind, take a long, deep breath and let it out slowly.

Do: Stay alert and conscious while you are relaxing. Pay close attention and note any changes in your body (feelings that stand out for you).

Don't: Allow yourself to become groggy and sleepy. If you start falling asleep, open your eyes and sit up. When you are ready, return to relaxation posture.

Do: Go at your own pace and let go of your muscles as your body decides to give up tension.

Don't: Expect yourself to relax all at one. Like any other physical exercise, you must practice letting go step by step.

Do: Give your body messages of appreciation for relaxing as you notice these feelings going through your body.

Don't: Get down on yourself for not relaxing. Your body should be trusted to go at its own pace.

Do: Stay award of your breathing. Observe how much air you're taking in full breaths at regular rhythms.

Don't: Smoke before, during or after relaxation as it tightens lung tissue and blood vessels. Let your body breathe.

Relaxation training technique

Record these directions for yourself by reading them slowly. Use the tape daily to practice the relaxation response:

Settle back as comfortably as you can and close your eyes. Let yourself relax to the best of your ability. Now, as you relax like that, clench your right fist. Just clench your fist tighter and tighter and study the tension as you do so. Keep it clenched and feel the tension in your right fist, hand, and forearm. Now relax. Let the fingers of your right hand become loose, and observe the contrast in your feelings. Now, let yourself go and try to become more relaxed all over. Once more, clench your right fist really tight Y hold it, and notice the tension again. Now let go, relax; your fingers straighten out and you notice the difference once more. Repeat that with your left fist. Clench your left fist while the rest of your body relaxes; clench that fist tighter and feel the tension. Now relax. Again, enjoy the contrast. Repeat that once more. Clench the left fist, tight and tense. Now do the opposite of tension: relax and feel the difference. Continue relaxing like that for a while. Clench both fists tighter and tighter, both fists tense, forearms tense. Study the sensations. Relax; straighten out your fingers and feel the relaxation. Continue relaxing your hands and forearms more and more.

Now bend your elbows and tense your biceps, tense them harder and study the tension feelings. Straighten out your arms, let them relax and feel that difference again. Let the relaxation develop. Once more, tense your biceps; hold the tension and observe it carefully. Straighten the arms and relax; relax to the best of your ability. Each time, pay close attention to your feelings when you tense up and when you relax. Now straighten your arms. Straighten them so that you feel the most tension in the triceps muscles along the backs of your arms; stretch your arms and feel that tension. Now relax. Get your arms back into a comfortable position. Let the relaxation proceed on its own. The arms should feel comfortably heavy as you allow them to relax. Straighten the arms once more so that you feel the tension in the triceps muscles; straighten them. Now concentrate on pure relaxation in the arms without any tension. Get your arms comfortable and let them relax further and further. Continue relaxing your arms even further. Even when your arms seem fully relaxed, try to go that extra bit further; try to achieve deeper and deeper levels of relaxation.

Let all your muscles go loose and heavy. Just settle back quietly and comfortably. Wrinkle up your forehead now; wrinkle it tighter. Now, stop wrinkling your forehead; relax and smooth it out. Picture the entire forehead and scalp becoming smoother as the relaxation increased. Now, frown and crease your brows and study the tension. Let go of the tension again. Smooth out the forehead once more. Now, close your eyes tighter and tighter. Feel the tension. Relax your eyes. Keep your eyes closed, gently and comfortably, and notice the relaxation. Now clench your jaws, bite your teeth together; study the tension throughout the jaws. Relax your jaws now. Let your lips part slightly. Appreciate the relaxation. Now press your tongue hard against the roof of your mouth. Look for the tension. Let your tongue return to a comfortable and relaxed position. Now purse your lips. Press your lips together tighter and tighter. Relax the lips. Note the contrast between tension and relaxation. Feel the relaxation all over your face, all over your forehead and scalp, eyes, jaws, lips, tongue and throat. The relaxation progresses further and further.

Now attend to your neck muscles. Press your head back as far as it can go and feel the tension in the neck now roll it to the left. Straighten your head and bring it forward. Press your chin against your chest. Let your head return to a comfortable position and study the relaxation. Let the relaxation develop. Shrug your shoulders. Hold the tension. Drop your shoulders and feel the relaxation. Neck and shoulders relaxed. Shrug your shoulders again and move them around. Bring your shoulders up and forward and back. Feel the tension in your shoulders and in your upper back. Drop your shoulders once more and relax. Let the relaxation spread deep into the shoulders, right into your back muscles; relax your neck and throat, and your jaws and other facial areas as the pure relaxation takes over and grows deeper, deeper, ever deeper.

Relax your entire body to the best of your ability. Feel that comfortable heaviness that accompanies relaxation. Breathe easily and freely in and out. Notice how the relaxation increase as you exhale. As you breathe out, just feel that relaxation. Now breathe right in and fill your lungs inhale deeply and hold your breath. Study the tension. Now exhale, let the walls of your chest grow loose and push the air out automatically. Continue relaxing and breathe freely, gently. Feel the relaxation and enjoy it. With the rest of your body as relaxed as possible, fill your lungs again. Breathe in deeply and hold it again. That's fine, breathe out and appreciate the relief. Just breathe normally. Continue relaxing your chest and let the relaxation spread to your back, shoulders, neck and arms. Merely let go. Enjoy the relaxation.

Now let's pay attention to your abdominal muscles; your stomach area. Tighten your stomach muscles, make your abdomen hard. Notice the tension. And relax. Let the muscles loosen and notice the contrast. Once more, press and tighten your stomach muscles, make your abdomen hard. Notice the tension. And relax. Let the muscles loosen and notice the contrast. Once more, press and tighten your stomach muscles. Hold the tension and study it, relax. Notice the general well being that comes with relaxing your stomach. Now draw your stomach in, pull the muscles in and feel the tension this way. Relax again, let your stomach out. Continue breathing normally and easily. Feel the gentle massaging action all over your chest and stomach. Now pull your stomach in again and hold the tension. Push out and tense like that; hold the tension. Once more, pull in and feel the tension.

Now relax your stomach fully. Let the tension dissolve as the relaxation grows deeper. Each time your breath out, notice the rhythmic relaxation both in your lungs and in your stomach. Try and let go of all contractions anywhere in your body. Now direct your attention to your lower back. Arch your back, making your lower back quite hollow, and feel the tension along your spine. Settle down comfortably again, relaxing the lower back. Just arch your back and feel the tension as you do so. Try to keep the ready of your body as relaxed as possible. Try to localize the tension throughout your lower back area. Relax once more, relaxing further and further. Relax your lower back, relax your upper back. Spread the relaxation to your stomach, chest, shoulders, arms and facial area, these parts relaxing further, further, further, ever deeper.

Let go of all tensions and relax. Now flex your buttocks and thighs. Flex your thighs by pressing down your heels as hard as you can. Relax and note the difference. Straighten your knees and flex your thigh muscles again. Hold the tension. Relax your hips and thighs. Allow the relaxation to proceed on its own. Press your feet and toes downward, away from your face, so that your calf muscles become tense. Study the tension. Relax your feet and calves. This time, bend your feet toward your face so that you feel tension along your shins. Bring your toes right up. Relax again. Keep relaxing for a while.

Keep relaxing more and more deeply. Make sure that no tension has crept into your throat; relax your neck and your jaws and all your facial muscles. Keep relaxing your whole body like that for a while. Let yourself relax all over.

Now you can become twice as relaxed as you are merely by taking in a deep breath and exhaling slowly. With your eyes closed you become less aware of objects and movements around you, thus preventing any surface tensions from developing. Breathe in deeply and feel yourself becoming heavier. Take in a long, deep breath and let it out very slowly. Feel how heavy and relaxed you have become.

In a state of perfect relaxation you should feel unwilling to move a single muscle in your body. Think about the effort that would be required to raise your right arm. As you think about raising your right arm, see if you can notice any tensions that might have crept into your shoulder and arm. You decide not to lift the arm but to continue relaxing. Observe the relief and the disappearance of tension.

Just carry on relaxing like that. When you wish to get up, count backward from four to one. You should then feel fine, refreshed, wide awake, and calm.

A full breathing exercise

Step 1: Lie prone on the floor. Loosen your belt and restrictive clothing.

Step 2: Relax and exhale as completely as possible. Begin to inhale slowly making your belly rise. Now move your rib cage. Now your chest. Hold it for a second. Now, exhale completely, all the air out of your lungs. Try it again. This is complete breathing. Breathe normally for a while, and in the next minute take at least one more complete breath. Pause one minute.

Step 3: You are still lying prone. As you lie there you will begin stretching muscles to achieve unblocked circulation. Bring your arms above your head and stretch them away from you fully. Now stretch your legs and feet downward, away from you, take a deep breath, let go and relax. Pause ten seconds. Feel the effects of the stretch on your body and on your breathing. Pause 15 seconds. Now sit up *very slowly*.

Step 4: Stand up for this part of the exercise. There are three very basic stretching postures to increase flexibility.

- backward bend

- forward bend

- side-to-side bend

As you do your backward bend pay attention to stretching your abdomen and back muscles. *Important:* Go only as far as you can. *Don't push yourself.* Bend slowly. As you do your forward bend, pay attention to the stretch of your back muscles and backs of legs; blood in head and arms. As you do your side stretch, pay attention to stretching in your chest, sides and neck.

Step 5: Assume a comfortable sitting posture, one you can hold for 15 to 20 minutes. This could be in a chair. Get comfortable and close your eyes when you are ready. *Please note everything you are aware of:* outside sounds, your bodily awareness, thoughts; note this awareness and do not change it. Then, notice shifting from outside sounds to thoughts of bodily awareness.

After approximately five minutes of this, notice that breathing is occurring; again, not to change it but only to notice it. One can enhance this noticing by attaching the words ``breathing out" to the breath as it leaves the nostrils and ``breathing in" as the breath reenters. As awareness shifts from breathing to thoughts of external sounds, allow that to happen and the return to ``breathing *out-breathing* in" (following the breath).

Continue this for five to seven minutes. At this point, try to incorporate some visual imagery in the form of a golden light with the *in-breath*. See yourself breathing in this golden light and watching it fill the inside of your body. This could be in a particle, vapor, smoke, or mist like form, whatever is comfortable for you. Visualize this light in your head, shoulders, chest and breath out any tensions in the form of a black color. Continue until you visually experience your whole body as being filled with this golden light. Experience that feeling.

Stay with this experience for another minute or two. Then, become aware of your breath again, with your body sitting on the floor or chair (feeling grounded). When ready, open your eyes.

Step 6: Try this breathing exercise for 15 to 20 minutes daily until you are able to achieve full breathing and stress reduction in a progressively shorter period of time.

Chapter # 9 — love yourself, and Take it Easy; Life is too Short

Love yourself; it is healthy; it is not selfish

How will anyone love you, if even you, don't love yourself? Just Love yourself; don't sabotage it, and you will Regain Joy of living

Some people feel that feeling bad and looking bad physically are proof that they are willing and able to pay and repent for their mistakes. We all have a set of values that we inherited from our childhood or from another source. Usually these values come from our religions, the traditions, social norms, and all the other beliefs we were exposed to.

Now is the time to look deep inside yourself and reevaluate all these beliefs (spiritual and non- spiritual values), and make some changes.

Some examples that you must change are:

1- I feel bad and guilty when I do things that my parents told me are sins. Our parents had good intentions when they told us that something was a sin (whatever it is), but we must think about what is good for us first without violating anybody's rights, and determining what violates others rights is a challenge in itself. Just use your common sense and love yourself anyways, because nobody else will love you if even you do not love yourself.

2- We subject ourselves to feeling guilty emotionally and as a result we suffer inside, and consequently we start to look bad physically. We think, unconsciously, that by suffering we pay our imaginary dues and the outside world (other people, God, etc) will see that we are suffering and they will know that we are paying the price. This is a myth, of course, because we are not serving any purpose by suffering; we are only hurting ourselves, and perhaps others also. Chances are that we are hurting the people who love us and whom we love. So, stop hurting yourself and start loving it. Do it anyways, even if it feels like you are selfish.

How to be successful and happy in your life

Ancient secrets:

Humans, from the beginning of time, strived to be happy and successful in their endeavors; many books were written on how to be happy and successful, and all the written books had only one common secret. You can be successful and happy if you know this ancient secret: Some things are under your power to control and some other things aren't. Your opinions and thoughts are your own, you can choose the actions you take, and you're always in charge of where you place your attention and focus. However, you don't have any say (control) over what goes on in someone else's head. So there's no way you can control another person's feelings or thoughts.

When you focus on the things you *can* control, you give yourself the gift of independence-you'll be unhindered and part of the natural flow of the universe and you empower yourself. By contrast, when you waste your energy on things you can't change, it inevitably weakens your sense of connection to the universal current (reality) and results in a sense of being enslaved and at the mercy of others. You play the role of the victim and you think somebody did this to me.

When you imagine that something is within your control when it isn't, you impede and disturb the natural flow of energy within and around you. You begin to blame others-even God-for what's happening to you. However, if you turn your attention toward the things that you can change, and withdraw your efforts from what you can't, then no one has any power over you. Nobody *can* hinder your progress toward getting what you want. You stop blaming those around you for your situation and you cease to do things you don't want to. Your enemies even fade away, believe it or not. Ultimately, no one can harm you because you don't let their actions affect you.

To achieve everything you want, it isn't enough to be just in part and a little bit motivated or partially committed. A halfhearted effort never works. For example, you can't just let go of your fears about other people's opinions of you some of the time, and you can't postpone taking charge of your life until a later date. If you want to be happy and free, you need to dive right in and take responsibility for the things under your control and let go of the things that aren't RIGHT NOW. Then, if you get off track, you need to recommit. Remember that it is your right to pursue happiness.

You are there, so do not give up

Many times people almost reach their goals, but right before they reach they abandon them; just like the gold digger who was searching for gold by digging deep into the ground, and as he was inches away from gold he stopped, and abandoned his digging and lost it all.

You must be patient and accept that everything worthwhile takes time.

Do not rush things because you are scared. Fear will only force you to make the wrong decisions. Consider every endeavor, small or big, as a project that has a beginning and an end- everything shall end and pass- in other words. Allocate just enough time to each project as you progress in accomplishing these projects.

You are a survivor because you have survived before and things shall pass, but be patient and do not rush things. Be patient when things get rough and tough; that's the real measure of your strengths and persistence, patience is a virtue as we all know.

You can make a difference by motivating yourself first or others

When you leave this world, you must ask yourself one question: What difference did I make? What's different now in this world because I was here on earth? And the answer to that question will be the difference that you made.

All of our intentions, thoughts, and feelings won't matter anymore when we are on our deathbeds asking that question. What will matter is the action we took and the difference that it made.

Yet we continue to obsess about our thoughts and become fascinated with our feelings. We are offended by other people. We want to prove we are right. We try to make other people look wrong. We are disappointed in some people and resent others. But, NOTHING except action will be all that matters at the end.

We could have made a difference every hour, every day, every month, and every year, if we had wanted to. So how do we do that? How do we motivate ourselves to get into action? How do we live a life of action difference-making?

The ancient philosophers, such as Aristotle, had the answer thousands of years ago: The answer lies in motion and action. The answer lies in movement, and not in lethargy. Just like the good old saying states: JUST DO IT. Aristotle knew, also, how to create a worthwhile self through movement and action. He once said this:

"Whatever we learn to do, we learn by actually doing it; *men* come to be builders, for instance, by building, and harp players by playing the harp: By doing self-controlled acts, we come to be self-controlled; and by doing brave acts, we become brave; Just act and live a life of action by simply effectuating and making things happen.

There is an old story that says in summary, and it categorizes people into three types: the first type is the few (unfortunately) people who are engaged and engrossed into making things happen and acting in general. The second type of people are the kind that simply stands by or sits down and watch others do things; they just WATCH what is happening in this world around them, and basically do nothing. The third type of people is the kind that ironically and unfortunately do nothing, nor do they even watch what is happening. In fact, they are the type that has no idea what is happening. This is the type that is totally lost and is wondering what the hell happened, when everything is all done and finished.

Energies we waste when we are angry-
Do not sweat the small stuff

Anger (when it is strong and intensive) as an emotion and feeling will usually make us feel victimized, revengeful, and makes us want to retaliate, and ultimately will engender and create a slew of other hurtful emotions. These emotions usually, if not controlled, may drain our energy and leave us fairly empty, lethargic, and drained of life's energy, and even sad and depressed.

The solution to all of these potentially lost energies is to:

1- not to fight for any matters that are trivial or beyond our control , just drop them and write them off and move ahead, and rise above the trivial people /events. Just do not sweat the small stuff.

2- Compromise and rise above pride, because pride does not solve problems, and when you compromise you will save your energy from being exhausted, sapped, and depleted.

3- Stand up only for the causes that really warrant the fight and be willing to negotiate for solutions. Remember, everything is negotiable except death, and never sweat the small stuff, because it is only small stuff.

Take life one day-at a time

Some simple mathematical calculations reveal some, perhaps to some of us, disturbing realities and facts, and here they are: If you live 100 years on this earth, that would be 36,500 days, or 876,000 hours ONLY on this lovely earth, and whether you like it or not you live sequentially- one day after the other, or a series of 36,500 days in series. So, do not try to cram too many tasks in one day, you will be overwhelmed and frustrated; life is not meant to be an overwhelming experience. As a baby, you had only one task, to eat, and sleep every day, and the goal was to survive. You did it very well. Today, it is really the same way of managing life; take every day as it comes- one at a time, tomorrow is not here yet. So wait to worry about tomorrow when tomorrow gets here. Cross that bridge when you get to it, as the adage goes. Enjoy yourself today and take it one day at a time, deal with what you can today, especially in hard times taking life one day at a time makes life simpler and easier, in other words livable with joy and passion.

Enjoy the moment: today, tomorrow, and the next day, and every day, because life itself is a big moment, and the moments of life are just a continuum of time and space, and a series of 24- hour intervals linked together to make up our life- a fleeting moment. Seize it and enjoy, revel in it.

Everything ends, whether it is good or bad

Keep in mind, always that fact, that indeed hard times pass, bad people die, or go away, or stop their abuse. Tomorrow you will be an adult like your dad, you make your own decisions and nobody will be able to abuse you. Nothing lasts forever, every event shall pass and life will go on. Do not despair because life is good, it is just that sometimes there are some setbacks, but life will be better when you work at it. Nothing happens in the vacuum, just keep doing the right things and the right results will be yours. It has been always cause and effect, your actions cause the effects (results).

Learn to negotiate with people and be prepared to compromise, but do not comprise your principles or compromise for the wrong reasons. Keep your integrity and compromise things that are negotiable; it is not the end of the world if you give or lose some material things, so be willing to compromise in this situation, for example when the loss is something you can live with and your life will continue without interruption, because it is all small stuff.

Fight fair when you have to fight back

Sometimes you have to defend yourself against various people.

Try to fight fair even when the fighter tries to be totally unfair to you, because it is the right thing to do. No matter what happened during the fight do not lower yourself down to a lower level some attackers stoop to.

Try to rise above the jealous, the envious, the simply vicious, the vindictive, and the bad person who attacks you and your ego and character. You know sometimes you have to return fire with fire…try to compromise because in any fight nobody wins, even if it seems that way.

Just keep going and do not let your attackers hurt you because if you do, you let them win twice: once when they attacked you and once more when they caused you to be hurt when you felt guilty or bad because of their attacks.

So just keep going and justice will prevail and you will be happy you did not let them hurt you.

Chapter # 10 — Learn to Think Clearly and Logically not Emotionally

Think clearly to You can Regain control of Your Life and Be Happy Again

Use your head not your emotions for clear thinking

When confronted by any situation that is problematic, use your head to address the problem and find a solution, even if your gut FEELINGS are to simply explode, for example. Use your logical mind instead of your emotions. Here are a few definitions of the methods and skills you should know.

CRITICAL THINKING:

Critical thinking is a decision –making process.

Critical thinking means carefully considering a problem, claim, question, or situation to determine the best solution.

Critical thinking (CT) helps you determine:

1) How to solve a problem.

2) To accept or reject a claim.

3) Answer a question.

4) Handle a situation.

REASONING SKILLS

Reasoning skills deal with the process of getting from point A (the problem) to point B (the solution).

A reason **is a** *motive* or *cause* for something – a justification for your thoughts, actions, opinions, etc. It is why you do, think, and say things.

Your reasons for doing things are not always reasonable – when you do or you say things under anger you do them based on your *emotions*, not reason (cause).

Creativity will help you reach success in your life

Creative people revel in making something out of nothing. Part of being creative is by setting goals. Most people who are successful in life are successful because they set goals and develop step-by-step action plans for achieving them. Unfortunately, only three percent of adults have clear, written goals. Especially considering that those who do accomplish up to 10 times more than other people, including people who are more talented. In fact, a person who sets goals - and focuses on taking small steps to achieve them - will run circles around a genius who talks a lot but never does anything. In fact about 36 percent of those who set New Year's resolutions give up by the end of January, and a full half of all resolutions are abandoned within three months. So, if you want to make this year your best creative year yet - and actually stick to your resolutions - it's time to set goals and adhere to them persistently. Do something that moves you closer to your goal; just do something, even very small, because it will add up and accumulate.

The power of goal setting:

What is true for the general and average population is also true for the creative people. There's only one way to ensure that hopes and dreams become real - and that's by setting goals. A goal is something you want, of course. But there's more to it than that. It's also something you're willing to work toward, whether it takes days, weeks, months, or years to achieve. In essence, goals are the stepping-stones that make your dreams become real.

Dream Big

Always dream big. Don't worry about whether you have the time, talent or money to achieve your dreams. Just write down whatever comes to mind. If you're having trouble completing your goals, imagine yourself 10 or even 50 years older. What if you only had six months to live? Think long-run, with a vision.

The size of your goals depends on the size of your dreams. Some goals can be achieved in a day, a week or a month. These are short-term goals. For example, taking a class on how to mix paint. Other goals - such as becoming a doctor or a business person can take much longer, perhaps years, even decades. These goals are called long-term goals. It's important to have both kinds of goals.

Setting Goals:

First: decide what you want.

The first step in setting your goals is to decide what you really want to focus your attention on, select about five things.

Second: write down your goals.

Once you've decided which five things you want to focus your attention on, the next step is turning each of them into a goal. Goals must be:

·Passionate: Passionate goals are easy to understand and use, and ignite your passion.

·Measurable: Measurable goals define the exact outcome you want to achieve: publish a book, complete a class in a specific area.

·Active: Active goals use "do it" words such as publish, draw and paint. They tell you exactly what it is you're supposed to do, rather than how it is you're supposed to feel.

·Reachable: Reachable goals are realistic. They can actually be achieved.

·Timed: Finally, your goals need deadlines, a specific time by which you'll achieve them: by noon on Friday, before my birthday, by December.

Now that you understand what makes a goal SMART, rewrite each of your goals making sure that it's savvy, measurable, active, reachable and timed.

Third: create an action plan

Now that you know exactly what it is that you want to accomplish, the next step is creating a step-by-step action plan for getting it. Break big goals into smaller goals, then think of each of your goals as the rungs of a ladder. Every small goal you complete means you climb one more rung on the ladder of your success. The more steps you take, the closer you are to the top - and to achieving the creative life of your dreams.

To develop your own goal ladder, make a list of all the things you need to do to reach your goal. Put them in order, beginning with the first step and so on, and give yourself a deadline for each step. And for good measure, share your goals and your action plan with someone you trust. Having someone else to whom you feel accountable will help you feel more accountable to yourself.

Celebrate your success

When you achieve a goal, celebrate your success. Buy a new DVD, Take a hot bath, schedule a weekend away. Better yet, enlist someone else who can help you. For instance, ask a friend to take you to a movie or treat you to lunch, or ask your partner to do the grocery shopping for the week or fill your car with gas for a month. And remember to reward yourself along the way, perhaps every time you climb another rung of your ladder. These rewards will fuel you to take the next step - and will help you stay focused on achieving your goals.

By following this process you'll no longer fret over and worry about failed resolutions. Instead, you'll be in the goal getters and achievers hall of fame.

Chapter # 11 — Your Funeral is tomorrow, So start living Today Live as if you are going to die tomorrow, because you might!

If I had my life to live over again

Someone who discovered suddenly that he had a serious deadly disease said: If I had my life to live over again, I would have talked less and listened more. I would have shared more of the responsibility carried by my spouse/ partner.

I would have cried- and laughed less while watching television and more while watching life.

Instead of wishing away nine months of pregnancy, I'd have cherished every moment and realize that the wonderment growing inside me was the only chance in life to assist God in a miracle. When my kids kissed me impulsively, I would never have said, "Later. Now, go get washed up for dinner." There would have been more "I love you's" More than "I'm sorry's." But mostly, given another shot at life, I would seize every minute...look at it and really see it... live it and never give it back. STOP SWEATING THE SMALL STUFF!!! Don't worry about who doesn't like you, who has more, or who's doing what. Instead, let's cherish the relationships we have with those who do love us.

Let's, think about what-God HAS blessed us with, and what we are doing each day to promote ourselves mentally, physically, and emotionally. I hope you have a blessed day.

10 SECRETS TO SUCCESS

Research has been conducted for many years analyzing leaders and successful people in all walks of life. The majority of these successful people and leaders have 10 common traits that, when combined, can turn dreams into reality. Here they are:

1. HOW YOU THINK IS EVERYTHING: Always be positive. Think success, not failure. Beware of a negative environment, and avoid its influence.

2. DECIDE UPON YOUR TRUE DREAMS AND GOALS: Write down your specific goals and develop a plan to reach them; DO NOT LEAVE YOUR FUTUTRE TO CHANCE AND OTHER FORCSES.

3. TAKE ACTION: Goals are nothing without action. Don't be afraid to get started. Just do it.

4. NEVER STOP LEARNING: Go back to school or read books. Get training and acquire skills.

5. BE PERSISTENT AND WORK HARD: Success is a marathon and lengthy, not a sprint or a tear. Never give up, unless you know there is evidence of success in sight- You see a dip you cannot bypass.

6. LEARN TO ANALYZE DETAILS: Get all the facts, all the input. Learn from your mistakes.

7. FOCUS YOUR TIME AND MONEY: Don't let other people or things distract you.

8. DON'T BE AFRAID TO INNOVATE; BE DIFFERENT: Following the herd is a sure way to mediocrity and the "USUAL".

9. DEAL AND COMMUNICATE WITH PEOPLE EFFECTIVELY: No person is an island. Learn to understand and motivate others.

10. BE HONEST AND DEPENDABLE; TAKE RESPONSIBILITY: Otherwise, Nos. 1-9 won't matter.